EXPECTING MOUNTAINS

Overcoming the Overwhelming Lows in Life

Shaunwell Posley

EXPECTING MOUNTAINS:
Overcoming the Overwhelming Lows in Life

Copyright

If you purchase this book without a cover, or purchase a PDF, jpg, or tiff copy of this book, it is likely stolen property or a counterfeit. In that case, neither the authors, the publisher, nor any of their employees or agents has received any payment for the copy.

Furthermore, counterfeiting is a known avenue of financial support for organized crime and terrorist groups. We urge you to please not purchase any such copy and to report any instance of someone selling such copies to Posley Global LLC.

This publication is designed to provide competent and reliable information regarding the subject matter covered. However, it is sold with the understanding that the author and publisher are not engaged in rendering legal, financial, or other professional advice. Laws and practices often vary from state to state and country to country and if legal or other expert assistance is required, the services of a professional should be sought. The author and publisher specifically disclaim any liability that is incurred from the use or application of the contents of this book.

Copyright © 2020 by Posley Global LLC. All rights reserved. Except as permitted under the U.S. Copyright Act of 1976, no part of this publication may be reproduced, distributed, or transmitted in any form or by any means or stored in a database or retrieval system, without the prior written permission of the publisher.

Published by Posley Global, LLC and 95Notes Publishing Group LLC are registered trademarks.

Printed in the United States of America

First Edition: 2020

ISBN: 978-1-7348994-7-4

EXPECTING MOUNTAINS:
Overcoming the Overwhelming Lows in Life
By Shaunwell Posley

Credits

Cover Art
by Youness El Hindami

Edited by
Michele L. Mathews
Olivia Gates
Shaunwell Posley

Photo by Theodor Lundqvist on Unsplash

To my daughter, Savannah Ariel Posley, and my wife, Asia Posley. My life changed upon your arrival in it. My mom, Lela Sue Washington and father, Robert Lee Posley Sr. You are my examples of excellence. My brother, Rob, you are the real ultimate warrior.

TABLE OF CONTENTS

Introduction	The Overview	9
Chapter One	The Mountain	19
Chapter Two	The Options Before You	37
Chapter Three	Climbing the Mountain	53
Chapter Four	Looking Back: R & C (Reflect & Celebrate)	69
Chapter Five	Climbing Down & Moving On	79
Chapter Six	The Bottom of the Mountain	91
Chapter Seven	Expecting Mountains	99
Chapter Eight	Another Mountain Awaits	137
Chapter Nine	The Next Level; Using your Past to Become a Greater You	147

Conclusion 153
About the Author 156
About the Publisher 158
My Paragons 159
YOUR Paragons 159
Valuable Notes Section 161

Introduction

THE OVERVIEW

"The tests we face in life's journey are not to reveal our weaknesses but to help us discover our inner strengths. We can only know how strong we are when we strive and thrive beyond the challenges we face."
–Kemi Sogunle

Life is tough. As humans, we experience unimaginable traumatic events that impact our lives and subconsciously influence our future. Our future is often unknowingly shaped by these unexpected events, and our survival depends on our ability to manage ourselves during these situations. Most people I have come in contact with often struggle with managing their scenarios. I have witnessed severe depression, self-harm, self-hate, and low self-awareness manifest as a result of the mishandling and misidentification of these life events. The ages of these individuals vary and could range from childhood to adulthood. Every living being experiences some kind of challenge, obstacle, or hardship as these things are expected, or, at least, they should be. How do you respond to your life challenges and hardships? Have you been depressed because of your past or due to the things that have taken place in your life? How do you overcome the overwhelming lows of life? This book supplies a recipe for overpowering life's challenges.

You are about to learn a concept that is game-changing and remarkable. This new way of thinking has been groundbreaking for the people who have applied its tenets and concepts to their lives. The individuals mentioned in this book are all real people I have encountered either as a student, employee, parent, and/or educator. This is the story of **Expecting Mountains: Overcoming the Overwhelming Lows in Life.** This book will help you make sense out of your everyday situations and life dilemmas. The idea of expecting mountains will transform your problems into adventures. This innovative way of thinking is the secret to finding control in an already out-of-control world. This new thought system is the key to changing your life around. Actually, this thought system is the key to realizing that your life has always been heading in the right direction, but this time as you progress on your journey, you will be in a position of complete control. The strategies presented in this book will assist you in identifying your already possessed talents and vast amount of already achieved accomplishments. The mountains of life are everywhere, so we must be prepared for them.

We are always surrounded by mountains. When I think back to my childhood, I can still hear the voice of my mother explaining the importance of understanding the natural lessons that life teaches us. I can vividly remember my mother saying, "A wise man never knows all, and only a fool knows everything." She advised to make sure to always learn and endure while on the journey through life. She told me at a very young age that keeping the mind open and positive was essential to becoming successful. She thought it was abundantly the essence of concern to grasp and soak up all of life's lessons while experiencing them.

As an adolescent boy, I never quite realized the impact and importance of her words. I never quite realized the importance of understanding that life's greatest teacher is experience itself. I didn't realize it at the time, but she was clearly experienced in climbing and overcoming life's mountains and thought it was necessary to pass her valuable life knowledge on to me. Like my mother, my father has been a mountain climber since birth.

As an African-American child, born in the South in the early 1950s, my father did not receive a common education. He was not properly educated like most African-Americans at the time, and as a result, he could not read. After moving to Chicago and attending a local elementary school, he met a one-of-a-kind third grade teacher. This wonderful educator sacrificed her personal time and stayed after-school every day to teach my father how to read. She grabbed his hand and helped him over his massive mountain. Due to the sacrifice of his teacher, my father eventually became the head radiologist for several of the leading medical facilities in Chicago. He has experienced many mountains and countless issues, but he exists as a strong being due to the journeys that he has experienced.

My grandfather was also an experienced mountain climber, not literally, but allow me to explain. My grandfather is the epitome of determination and resilience due to his innate ability to climb and overcome mountains. When my grandfather was eight years old, sometime between the years of 1936 and 1937, a private airplane crashed into his house, killing his mother (my great-grandmother) and uncle. He was the only member of his family that was spared. His mother and uncle were his only caretakers at the time, and because of this tragedy, he had to learn how to survive life on his own. A family friend took him in and raised him. As a young boy, despite the severe pain and massive trauma that he experienced, my grandfather climbed along and kept moving. As part of his bounce back plan, he joined the army at the age of twelve and married my grandmother when he was fourteen. He opened and owned an exterminating business, managing to become very successful, especially for an African-American male living in the U.S. during the tumultuous 1950s. Life threw mountains, and my grandfather climbed and climbed and climbed. All of these stories served as examples in my life of how to journey over mountains.

I have also had an exciting life despite the many mishaps and mistakes made along the way. I entered the workforce at the age of nine and have been in it ever since. I have come to know many people throughout my twenty-five years of work experience. I have worked in various fields, which provided phenomenal opportunities to interact with many people. Despite working in many different sectors throughout my life, I decided to follow one of my life's dreams and become an educator in 2012. During my journey into the field of education, I experienced tremendous struggles on a daily basis.

I faced lots of adversity in pursuit of both, my bachelor's and master's degrees. While chasing success, I never gave up and stayed focused on my journey. I forced myself to learn and ascend through every step of the process. I wanted to prove that even if your journey seems impossible and if you stay focused, you will succeed at your goals. Everything can be as simple as it sounds. Face your mountains, climb your mountains, and complete the vital routes of your journey to become a successful you, just as my grandfather did. I successfully attained both degrees becoming a first-generation graduate despite my background and upbringing in the rough streets of Chicago during the vicious and violent 1990s. My destination is not determined by my location as I will find success even if it's in a box. To fully grow and reach success, it was important to discover exactly how to become the greatest me. Expecting and understanding mountains is essential to pushing past the average you and finding the greatest you.

Sometimes in life, our stories, our experiences, and our journeys are the things that are helping us to become who we are. It's important to take every lesson in life seriously to progress. You need your life experiences to mold you into the person you are to become. These life experiences are often not a bed of roses that grow without maintenance or a sunny beach filled with coconut trees blowing in a cool ocean breeze. Sometimes these experiences force you awake at night. These life situations are not presented as gifts of enjoyment.

NO.

Sometimes, life throws mountains at us, and other times, we are thrown helplessly at the foot of a mountain. So, imagine yourself down at the bottom of a mountain. As you approach this mountain, think about what your options are.

OPTION 1:

You can turn around and **run away** from the mountain, but when you return, the mountain will still be there waiting for you – wondering where you have gone but definitely still there waiting for your return.

OPTION 2:

You can approach the mountain and just **stand** at the mountain's feet, staring at it and **complaining** about it being a mountain, extremely upset that it is there. Pride forces complaint-filled questions to be screamed directly at the mountain's base. "Mountain, why are you here?" "Mountain, why today?" and "Mountain, why me?" These sets of words do nothing to the mountain. The complaints do not and will not help progress, so why complain? Why waste time wondering about things that do not matter in the long run? The only thing that matters in the short and/or long run is the mountain.

OPTION 3:

You can go around the mountain, attempting to **avoid** it, but this can be dangerous. In addition, when you go around the mountain, you will waste too much time, and you may get lost or go too far off the trail.

OPTION 4:

You can **climb up** the mountain! When you climb up the mountain, a lot of natural reactions begin to happen as your mind and body becomes stronger. Therefore, you become stronger – its basic science. We cannot tell our bodies to resist becoming stronger when it is exercising. It will become stronger no matter what! The same thing happens to the mind and body when climbing mountains.

Of course, you will encounter pain, and you will definitely experience fatigue. Your journey up the mountain will be difficult, but when you reach the top of the mountain, you will become stronger naturally.

Understand that mountains represent the obstacles in your life. The mountain represents every bad situation, complication, or hiccup that you encounter in the course of life. The mountains of life are always approaching, and it is up to you to choose how to react to these obstacles. Every time you encounter a mountain, even if the mountain seems impossible to overcome, you are obliged to choose from these said options, and it is up to you to decide if you will or will not allow the mountain to defeat you.

This book teaches you how to take control of your situation and how to destroy any obstacle that stands before you. An individual can either conquer their obstacles or fall prey to a state of suffering. Author Jake Smith, in his book, *10 Steps to a Happier Life*, rightly stated, "You have the choice to wallow in misery, to continue to let life happen to you, to take control of your life, and even the choice to decide how you will view or react to the bad things that will happen along the way." It is up to you to decide how to react to your hardships because they are coming and can care less if you are ready for them. These devastating situations can be huge mountains or minuscule molehills, but they are definitely headed to a theater near you.

This book will provide strategies to assist in handling life's difficulties, obstacles, and problems as they are thrown your way. I created this tactical way of thinking at a moment in life when I was facing difficult times. My problems were everywhere I looked, and I was beginning to feel buried by them. My problems infiltrated my finances, relationships, and personality. At this time in my life, I hated my job, hated my circumstances, and was beginning to hate myself. My wife, who I was dating at the time, was extremely frustrated and disappointed at the person that I allowed my problems to make me become.

At this point, I decided to change my perception, recalculate my perspective, and listen to the words of my mother. I invented this way of thinking to change my perceptions and control my direction. Little did I know that

I created a thinking mechanism that would change everything about my life. I have seen my bank account climb all the way from negative amounts to figures beyond my imagination. My relationship with my wife could not be any better, and it is all due to the idea and understanding of the *mountain philosophy*. I am currently a multiple award-winning educator. I own multiple businesses and publish major authors, poets, and artists from all over the world through 95Notes Publishing Group, and most notably, I was recruited by Scholastic Art & Writing Awards as a juror (an honor and seat once held by Langston Hughes and many others). The list of accomplishments continues. I have never felt so happy and could not have done it without my knowledge of overcoming mountains. When I became a teacher, after experiencing student after student suffering from *mountain overload*, I added all of the elements together to create this theory.

This book is a tool that can be used to guide you through the journey of overcoming life's mountains, and it provides proven methods of how to get the best out of life's bad situations.

Life has thrown you a lemon. It is time to throw that damn lemon back. Come on this journey and let's explore our mountains together, discovering ways to successfully get over them while readying ourselves for mountains that follow.

Chapter One

THE MOUNTAIN

"Everyone wants to live on top of the mountain, but all the happiness and growth occurs while you are climbing it."
– Andy Rooney

Have you ever wondered why people climb mountains as a hobby? How can people find it in their hearts and minds to justify this dangerous activity of climbing mountains. Most of the time, these adventurers must step over or walk around the dead bodies of other people who have engaged in the exact activity that they are currently engaging in. For example, nearly 300 people have died trying to climb the world's tallest mountain, Mount Everest. People die every year on this mountain and the last year on record that a person was not documented to have died on the mountain was all the way back in 1977. During that year, only two people set their feet on the crown of the mountain. All of the dead bodies of the hikers who did not make it are still scattered throughout Mount Everest. The hikers request for their bodies to be left on the mountainside if something should happen as it follows the same understanding as a captain going down with his ship. They believe it to be an honor to die doing what they love. On Everest, the renowned body of an unidentified hiker only known as Green Boots is now used as a guidepost for other adventurers as they travel. This unidentified body is known because he is wearing a pair of neon green boots. Some hikers even take selfies once they reach this unnatural marker on the mountain.

I know stepping over and around dead bodies is pretty gross, right?

So why do people climb mountains in the first place? There must be something about climbing mountains that is so enticing that people ignore all *rational* thoughts and consciously choose to embark on this dangerous quest.

According to actual mountain climbers, not only is climbing mountains fun, but the main thrill is said to be achieved once you reach the top of the mountain's summit. It is reportedly one of, if not, the best feeling in the world. Think about riding to the top of the tallest Ferris wheel that your mind can imagine. Now multiply that feeling by one million. However, if you happen to be afraid of heights, don't imagine this scene at all.

Whether the mountain is tall like Everest or just a few thousand feet tall, reaching the summit gives a huge sense of accomplishment. Even the pictures taken from mountaintops show how wonderful an experience of getting to the top of the mountain can be, but this is nothing compared to actually being up there and witnessing it yourself. Imagine watching a video of the sun rising versus experiencing this wonderful phenomenon with your own eyes. There's no comparison.

Yes, climbing mountains is a rather hard and dangerous hobby, but that only makes the experience more enjoyable. In life, it is suggested to take calculated risks. People often associate risk with death and would rather play it safe. Safe usually keeps you in place and gets you nowhere! Why cross the street when it is safer to stay at home? Why go swimming when it is safer to stay on land? Why ride a bicycle when it is safer to sit at home on the couch, daydreaming about leaving the house? The list of safe analogies could go on and on, and trust me, I could go on forever. Sometimes, it is the risks in life that make living worthwhile.

Risk management should be your greatest asset. The great boxer and activist, Muhammad Ali, once said, "He who is not courageous enough to take risks will accomplish nothing in life." Life, as we know it, is an excursion, and we are all soldiers on this expedition either taking risks or hiding from opportunities. We are all headed somewhere, and while some of us have a clue where our journey leads, many of us are lost not possessing any clue about which direction to go. Sometimes an individual breaks out of the status quo, takes their destiny into their own hands, and makes strong efforts to determine where their journey is going. Other times, life, also like Muhammad Ali, punches us in the face and knocks us off of our path.

As we embark on life's journey, one thing is a guarantee. There will be good times followed by bad times, and it is important to understand how to handle your interactions with your world. There has not been any human being that has come in contact with this earth that has not encountered one form of difficulty in life at one time or another. We call these situations, *mountains*, and while some people go out and seek their own mountains to climb, others have mountains thrusted into their faces. Most of these events occur at times when they are not-at-all prepared for it. These mountains come in many different shapes and forms and cut across all spheres of our lives whether it is educational, work-related, family-orientated, or relationship-based, but one thing is for sure. A person must overcome, get past, and get over their problems to move forward in life.

I have encountered, encouraged, and advised thousands of people throughout my twenty-five years of work history and almost matched years of schooling. I have met, managed, and interacted with some amazing individuals. I have been impressed and impacted by the stories that I have come across throughout the years. However, I am usually concerned with the *head*-down sadness that always seem to accompany stories about life's obstacles as if everyone with a pulse has not experienced their own set of issues, has not encountered their own massive mountain, or has not experienced their own wave of worries. Some of the most successful people of all times have experienced extremely treacherous mountains. These problems should not be spoken about with great disdain or regret. The real question is easy. What do you do when you are looking at your mountain? What do you do when you are standing at the bottom of a mountain?

A very close friend of mine experienced a range of mountains at an early age. I first met Benjamin Baker, as we will call him, when I was in the second grade as we, in the most gangster of ways, rolled marbles back and forth in class with each other. I'm not too sure why Ben brought marbles to school in the first place, but we briefly enjoyed this rather dangerous and risky game in the middle of class instruction, laughing each time the teacher turned her back as we rolled the tiny ball back and forth across the classroom. Sometimes we increased our opportunity for peril by adding another marble to join in our game of Marble Mayhem. This was the first sign that Ben was definitely a risk-taker. This interaction was one of my first memories of Ben as this eruption of fun caused a major class disruption and resulted in both of us getting disciplined by the teacher followed by a not-so-funny phone call home. However, this would not be my friend's last time sailing close to the wind as he learned how to remain in trouble for most of his adolescent years. As a matter of fact, Ben might as well have been named trouble. Ben was handed a childhood complete with problems and pain. As we grew older, Ben acted out in and out of school and showed the signs of his struggles as he ambled through life. Ben's father was shot and killed when he was five years old. Ben wore this pain as a badge of shame and never faced it. When Ben was about seven, his uncle abused him. He also wore this abuse as a badge of shame, and he never faced it. When Ben was about thirteen, he committed a misdemeanor crime and was taken into juvenile custody. Likewise, he equally wore this circumstance as a badge of shame and never faced it.

Benjamin never expected his life to go anywhere, so it never did. Ben allowed the pains that he encountered early in life to control his directions later in life. He allowed life's obstacles to control his existence. Ben never faced his mountains. Instead, he avoided them, complained about them, and ran away from them.

One day when we were much older, Ben contacted me, and we met up and had an in-depth discussion about life, career, relationships, and pretty much anything else that mattered. At one point, he told me about being worried that he would never be able to find a decent job because nothing positive ever happened in his life. He said nothing ever goes right in his world and he has never gotten the things that he's wanted. He went on saying that he never received anything good from his mother or father, and he blamed them for his circumstances. He didn't think that he should even try to look for a job. He didn't want to feel the rejection. He didn't want to face his obstacles. Ben made excuses for his circumstance, not realizing that he was in this position only because he was most comfortable in this position of victimhood. Yes, his childhood was full of misfortune, but it was *his* childhood. Ben's life was full of obstacles, and he suffered due to the way he responded to what life was giving him.

I told Ben to use his past as a springboard or pogo stick –to be always moving forward. "You must use your past as the fuel needed to drive you to success. You have to!" I instructed. Just like a video game, we have to learn to level up and improve each day. Normally, in a video game, you begin playing as the main character at his or her most undeveloped state, and as you progress by the end of the game, you are usually all powerful. The thing is that we have to get better with each moment. With every breath taken, your next breath should be better. We must improve ourselves just as we improve our characters in video games.

I advised Ben that he still had an opportunity to be successful, but he needed to face his mountains. He needed to level up. I believed that Ben was extremely depressed and angry about his circumstances, which resulted in his misuse of life's fuel that got in the way of his success. He needed to **become** stronger by facing, climbing, and overcoming his mountains. Ben was very receptive while receiving this information. Ben understood the *mountain concept* because he was used to mountains. Actually, he was too used to mountains appearing around him. His biggest problem was that he did not know what to do when he ran into these mountains. I told him that I recently overcame my problems in the same fashion. I broke down the *mountain concept*, at least at its infant stages, as at this time, the theory was not yet fully developed.

Of course, Ben did not get it together right after our conversation. Information is just words until the action happens. Plans are just words on paper until a person actually applies the necessary vision. Actively applying knowledge is a necessary component of true learning. So Ben continued at his losing streak until that one day he decided to face his mountains and go through the *process* that would eventually become the solution to helping him prevail past his obstacles. The *process* is necessary for chasing success and defeating comfort. Ben's first major uncomfortable decision was to go to counseling, and this decision was life-changing. I do not believe that it was necessarily the counseling or the counselor that made the most impact on Ben's life. However, I do believe that it was his decision to go through his *process* by performing the *uncomfortable*. He performed the *uncomfortable* by completing a positive action in which he would never do. He sacrificed his comfort in search for greatness.

Ben finally decided to face his mountain, and that decision changed his life. Today, Ben is a hugely successful salesman for a Fortune 500 firm. He was able to realize his talents. He became a strong salesman because of his past and his knowledge of what to do when faced with problem after problem. Ben began to understand that life is filled with setbacks, especially while on your way up the mountain, but these situations are just that—setbacks. Rejection was initially one of Ben's setbacks that eventually became his asset because as a salesman, being afraid of rejection is poisonous to success. He learned and figured out the purpose of mountains and the necessary steps needed to conquer his experiences. He turned his poison into power. Ben understood the power of mountains and the excitement of the experience. Benjamin applied the idea of expecting mountains into every aspect of his life.

Can you relate with Ben? Are you having trouble dealing with life right now because every time you look up, there is a problem knocking at your door? Does it feel like every time you decide to look out the window, there is a mountain blocking your sights?

Are you a student having a difficult time balancing school and work, school and home life, or school and sports? Or is your primary problem the lack of money to pay for the increasing cost of education and textbooks? Are student loans knocking at your door? These are the situations in life that appear as mountains.

Do you have a family member to take care of, but you just don't make enough money at your job or can't seem to get that promotion you have been hoping for that will eventually help to offset your bills? These are the obstacles in life that appear as mountains.

Are you a person plagued with the problem of substance abuse, and the more you try to stay away from using them, the more you are attracted to using them? Addiction is your mountain to overcome.

Or you are a single mother catering to the needs of your child while at the same time trying to better yourself and get a degree, so you have to find a balance between your child, your classes, and your job? Management of your life is your steep mountain to overcome.

Is your mountain depression? Is your mountain sickness? Is your mountain heartbreak? Is your mountain the loss of a loved one? The list goes on and on, but it definitely doesn't stop. The mountains of life will continue to come, and news flash, they are not concerned about your feelings.

The more a person lives, the more mountains they will encounter. It is a seemingly inevitable fact that as a living being, you are guaranteed to experience hardship. At times, life can seem so complicated that problems appear to be everywhere you turn. It's like one obstacle after another. Sometimes it can seem like there are more mountains than valleys; however, how you handle these mountains once they are encountered is entirely up to you.

An individual who faces many obstacles become toughened by their encounters. So, obstacles are not always as bad as they may seem. Rather, they teach you how to survive and how to endure. They build up your endurance and resilience.

Sometimes when I order fragile packages from Amazon or UPS, they come with the highlighted instructions, "*Handle with Care*," written directly in red on the top of the box or envelope. These packages must be labeled this way because if they are not properly labeled, there is a strong likelihood that the package will be damaged and/or broken. Humans who rarely face any hardships in life may need to be treated the same as these tender-to-touch packages because they may be as fragile as the items inside of the "handle-with-care box." These fragile people might have the tendency to easily crack under pressure since the more mountains that you encounter in life, the tougher you become. So enjoy your experience with pain, being that this valuable interaction makes a person more durable with a higher endurance level in the long run.

Let me detail the story of how I fully developed the *Mountain Theory*, which happened during my second year of teaching ninth grade high school students. No, the theory of expecting mountains was not for me because of the difficulty of teaching high school students even though it should have been.

As a teacher, when I began each school year, I usually began with individual questions for each student, during which I instruct that they must answer any question asked because it is a class rule that, "I don't know," or not answering a question is a response that is not allowed at all. During this class initiation process, I would fire off questions as I called their names for attendance: "Johnny Sanders, if you can be an animal, what would you be?" "Rebecca Santos, what do you expect to learn this year?" "Emmanuel Jackson, what do you want to do when you are older?" This process usually goes on for the first few weeks or at least until we have gotten to know each other better.

I usually receive amazing responses, and sometimes answers can be rather silly. However, in this process, my method of "madness" is to inspire the students to use their voices, and this process also allows me to learn a lot about their dreams and interests. When I get to the last question about their future plans, I write their responses down in a notebook, recording each one as they are given to me. I always make sure that they notice me writing each one down to hold each student accountable for their dreams as long as we know each other. I normally receive responses like, "I want to be in the NBA," "I want to be a nurse," and/or "I want to be a veterinarian." Their responses can be entertaining, charming, and innovative.

However, during my second year of teaching while I was carrying out this process, I met a student that stressed how she was unable to answer this question. She told me that she didn't have any dreams. For confidentiality purposes, we will call this student, Samantha Davis. Sam told me she did not want to be anything because she believed she could not be anything. She believed life had already decided that she was to be nothing. She told me that at the early age of thirteen, based on the current circumstances in her life, life had already made its decisions about her future and there was nothing that she could do about it.

You see, Sam experienced an extremely difficult childhood. Growing up, she faced so many obstacles, and Sam believed that judgment in life was based on her then present circumstances and the obstacles that were put before her. She felt as if she was, in a way, cursed. She lived with foster parents after being abused by a close family member for years, and she was ashamed of her experiences. Sam was also ashamed that she had foster parents, so she kept her adoption story a secret from even her closest friends. Sam was embarrassed by her story, so she held her story close. Sam's foster parents attempted to care, but she had a hard time trusting people. Plus, they had three other children, so Sam felt she was an extra burden to such a nice and innocent family. Samantha blamed her life circumstances on her existence and felt bad things happened because they had to happen, so she expected them to happen. Sometimes when the bad did not happen, she made bad happen.

I discovered Samantha's story after I became her mentor, which was an extremely difficult process, as I stated that she rarely trusted in any individuals. After speaking with Sam after class and through thorough interaction, explaining the story of how life is about expecting mountains, detailing Ben's life story as well as mine, and making sure that the lessons of the mountain were being applied to her life, Sam now dreams regularly. Samantha understood and applied the lessons of the mountain to her life. Sam is currently a senior in college and could very well be a graduate by the time you are reading this story. All of my interactions indirectly assisted in the creation of this thought system, but Samantha's situation directly inspired the entire idea because I needed a relatable metaphor to use that would help Samantha and then other students/people understand the purpose of life's difficulties.

Are you like thirteen-year-old Sam or early Ben? Do you think your life is the worst? Do you believe your story is so painful that you would rather keep it all inside and shy away from confronting your mountains? What do you do when you are faced with mountains? Do you throw in the towel? What if you threw in the towel well before you were even in the ring? Do you often quit before climbing your mountain? Do you give up before you even get to realize your moment of control? What if you have been giving up way too early? Sam could be you at any moment in your life, whether thirteen, thirty, or fifty.

What mountain is presently before you? What obstacle seems insurmountable in your life? Remember, even the smallest dream appears unachievable at the initial stages, and the majority of the world's most successful people encountered and had to overcome some incredible obstacles at some point in their life. So, you are not the first to experience hardship. It is important, that despite all of the obstacles encountered, you must still continue to dream. When I met Samantha, she said her past caused nightmares, so she couldn't dream anymore. She did not want to dream anymore. You must make sure that despite how difficult the climb, you continue to want everything that is on the other side. If anything, the obstacles encountered during the process of achieving success are part of what makes the journey more fulfilling, more rewarding, and more satisfying.

    You must develop the right mindset about the mountains in your life. Author of *The Greatest Salesman in the World*, Og Mandino, rightfully declares that "failure would never overtake one if the determination to succeed is strong enough." Your will to succeed can make you invincible. Yes, it's all about your attitude when you encounter these problems. If you think you can't overpower your problems, you will end up not overpowering your problems. If you think you will fail, you have already started failing, and the result of your thinking will not be so different than your thought process. A winning mindset is key to successfully climbing any type of mountain that you encounter in your life. Hiking, they say, is one of those things that you can only do when you have the determination in you. So get ready for the mountains of life because they are sure to come. What are you going to do when they arrive and you are standing at the bottom of your mountain? What are your options, and which one do you choose?

Chapter Two

THE OPTIONS BEFORE YOU

"Life presents you with so many decisions. A lot of times, they're right in front of your face, and they're really difficult, but we must make them."
– Brittany Murphy

You have identified your mountain and the next step is all about your reaction when being faced with this giant issue. Pay very close attention because your reaction to the mountain you are facing will go a long way in determining how your life will turn out. A lot of persistent problems in life are ones that could have easily been solved if the correct decisions were made when the problems initially arose. Decisions like these, just Brittany Murphy accurately stated, are sometimes really tough, but despite everything, we are still required to make them.

There are several options available when faced with a mountain, and they are as follows:

OPTION 1: YOU CAN TURN AROUND AND RUN AWAY FROM THE MOUNTAIN.

Running away from the mountain is by far the easiest option of them all, and it's based on the idea that you are running away from the issues in life. A lot of people easily go for this option, but I can guarantee that this option is, not in any way, shape, or form, the best way to solve the problems that come into our lives. Easy options should always be carefully approached and analyzed. Many times they come with huge drawbacks, mostly because of the lack of effort needed to make progress. My mother always used to say, "When you run away from all of your problems, you eventually run away from yourself." By running away from the mountain, you are avoiding the necessary steps of the journey to becoming the ultimate you.

NBA great and billionaire, Michael Jordan, was faced with one of his life-deciding mountains as a sophomore in high school. The only reason why the name, Michael Jordan, even sounds a bit familiar is because of his decision to not run away from the massive mountain that he faced at a crucial time in his life. Although you may have heard this story before, allow yourself the opportunity to look at it from another perspective. In 1978, the great MJ did not make the varsity basketball team despite being pretty good. I mean, he is, Jordan, but was he actually his true self at this time before approaching this mountain? Unfortunately (but fortunately for Jordan), he was not tall enough at the height of 5'10" and did not meet the vision of the coach. Jordan reportedly looked at the tryout list of prospects posted on the high school's gym door after trying out for his high school team, and to his surprise, his name was not listed. Jordan did not make the basketball team. As a result of being overlooked and devastated, he went home, locked himself in the bathroom, and reportedly cried for two long hours. Luckily, (because I am a Chicago native and witnessed his greatness), Jordan entered the bathroom broken but exited the bathroom a different person. Jordan did not stay in the bathroom in fear of the next steps, hiding from the mountain of defeat. At that moment, he decided to work harder and become better. He opened the door hungrier than when he went in, and this has nothing to do with the fact that he was in the bathroom for two hours. Jordan soared over a very important mountain. Has the real you gone in hiding, locked the door, and stayed inside too long in fear of the shadows of your mountain?

Of course, it is said that he who fights and runs away, lives to fight another day, but that is for people who have fought in the first place. This idea doesn't apply when you have not attempted to fight and when you have not tried to climb your mountain.

This is the same scenario that usually unfolds when faced with school bullies. You can keep running away from and avoiding them, but what does that do? Most of the time, it makes the situation worse and invigorates the confidence of the bullies, and the bullies become more aggressive. Almost every movie with a bully plot addresses this issue of passivity or *mountain retreating* with a final confrontation that places the bullied in a head-on collision with the bullies, and the confrontation almost always solves the problem for the so-called victim. I know that Hollywood productions are not the final answer for receiving credible information, but I have also witnessed this bully situation play out with my own eyes as a teacher.

You can run away from your mountain as much as you like, but whenever you return, the mountain will still be there, still waiting for you – wondering where you have gone. No matter how far you run away from your mountains, they will still be exactly where you left them. Think like Michael Jordan was thinking when he unlocked the door of the bathroom and walked out to address the world. At least, he opened the door, still wounded, but brave enough to address the issue at hand.

In order to get ahead, you must move past the mountains of your life and advance to the next level as it is impossible to achieve this by running away from your mountains. Again, it is like leveling up in any video game that allows you to do so. You cannot spend your entire life as a default character or in the same mental position you started in. You can't possibly spend the rest of your life running from the problems that are guaranteed to be waiting to confront you. You can never take a break from your problems, so stop asking for one.

These problems and life's dilemmas are something you cannot run from. A vivid example of this idea in action is the story of Jonah in the Bible. God called Jonah to preach to the people of Nineveh because they were too wicked – this was his calling. However, Jonah hated this idea because he didn't want to have anything to do with the Israelites, who were considered one of the greatest enemies of his people. So what did Jonah do? Jonah decided to run from his calling (mountain), and instead of following his path, he ran away by boat in the opposite direction to a place called Tarshish. This caused him to experience more difficulties on his journey while running away from his problems. Instead, he only wasted his time. During the journey, there was a massive storm, and he was thrown into the river when it was revealed that his *mountain retreating* was causing the sea storm. After going overboard, Jonah was swallowed by a whale in whose belly he stayed for three days. Eventually, Jonah was thrown ashore at Nineveh, which is the same place he had run away from, and he went on to fulfill his calling by preaching to the Israelites.

By comparing Jonah and the mountain retreaters, we can see that a lot of us are just like Jonah. Some of us go for the easy option of running away from our problems instead of facing them head-on. As a result of picking the easy way, we go through unnecessary stress, take unneeded steps, and cause mental uncertainty because no matter what, the problem still exists. We still will have to come back and face the problem eventually, just like in the case of Jonah. So we must be like Jordan, Jonah, Ben, and Sam and realize that Option 1 is just not an option.

OPTION 2: YOU CAN APPROACH THE MOUNTAIN BUT JUST TO STAND AND COMPLAIN ABOUT ITS EXISTENCE.

Any person who has a pulse is guaranteed to run into mountains in their life. Some people will choose the second option instead of the first one, but this time, they will stand at the mountain's feet, staring at it and complaining about it being a mountain. They are upset that the problem is there. These people will complain about their problems and play the role of victim. They question why the obstacles have the audacity to be in their lives, asking questions like, "Mountain, why are you here?" "Mountain, why today?" and "Mountain, why me?" When this option is selected, it doesn't come alone as it brings along its friends—depression, low self-awareness, and low self-esteem with it. This option forces the mountaineer to complain and compare their lives to the lives of others. They wonder why they are the only ones going through hell. Their complaints are usually widespread and irrational.

It is a good thing they took that first step of approaching their mountain. Yes, that should be applauded, but what happens after confronting the mountain? Nothing positive! They just stand there and complain, not making any progress in their journey toward success and absolutely no progress in, ultimately, overcoming their mountain.

At this moment, it is important to point out that nagging about a problem has never been a solution to overcoming any issue that stands before you. Complaining will not move the mountain and talk without action will not get anyone anywhere. Complaining does nothing to the mountain because without positive ascension, the mountain will still be there. Without action, the mountain will still be a mountain. Without a solution, the problem is still a problem. So, why waste time and energy complaining about something that doesn't really care or plan to do anything about the complaint?

Imagine a scenario where you are on a journey, and along the way, you come upon a huge rock blocking your path. You head over to the huge boulder, and instead of doing something about it, you just stand there, shouting at the boulder and asking, Who put this right in the middle of my pathway?

First, it is safe to assume that you have lost your mind, but mostly, we can assume your journey ends right there at the beginning of the mountain or your journey will be on hold at least until a forward action takes place because the obstacle will not go anywhere if you just stand there and complain about it.

This is the same thing that happens when dealing with problems in life. Most of the time, we wonder and search for the reasons why things happen in our life. Somehow, we have convinced ourselves that we are not supposed to go through anything that is unplanned, and when we experience any troubling situation, these experiences almost always trouble us. We feel that we deserve so much better. We feel entitled to having good experiences, but guess what? These troubling experiences or mountains keep coming! It is only right that we get used to the ideas of mountains and stay away from the all too self-righteous option of complaining about the problems in our lives when they show themselves. Instead of standing there complaining, you should do something about it because actions have spoken and will always continue to speak louder than words. Jordan used his heartbreak to propel himself into the record books of our lives. He did not complain about the mountain for a third hour while he was locked into the bathroom. Neither should you.

OPTION 3: YOU CAN GO AROUND THE MOUNTAIN IN AN ATTEMPT TO AVOID IT.

On the surface, this is another seemingly smart option, but in reality, it is not so smart. When confronted with life's problems, some people will turn and run. Some people will stand, stare, and complain about the problems before them while others will avoid them altogether. Avoiding a problem is only a temporary solution. This solution is momentary because nothing has been done to address the overlaying issue, and even though you did not entirely turn and run away from the problem, you are still not so different from the people who do.

Avoiding is a form of running. However, it is running around instead of running away.

Yes, great, the problems are now behind you, but due to the fact that you did not address them, they are now chasing you. Unfortunately, the problems will not disappear.

It is also important to note that when trying to find ways around problems, usually more time is spent, and more resources are wasted looking for shortcuts than if an individual had just confronted the problem head-on. Many people use more energy searching for shortcuts than searching for solutions. This happened recently while I was driving when I did not want to use my navigation system because I assumed I knew where I was. While searching for a shortcut, I ended up thirty minutes off track wasting lots of gas, looking for a quicker solution to the already known solution. This happens on actual roads but also takes place on the roads of life.

So, what happens when a person successfully avoids their mountain? They usually sense slight satisfaction, but this is short-lived because their mountain will still be there. More importantly, the problem will still be unsolved. My childhood friend, Ben, was momentarily satisfied each time he avoided his life issues. Remember the scenario previously mentioned that involved the rock blocking your only path? Let's imagine trying the option of going around the boulder or avoiding the obstacle altogether.

By taking this option, you will waste more time and much more energy searching for a way to avoid dealing with it. I can imagine a pretty damaged car or ending up lost and out of gas like myself when I tried to take the shortcut. By going off the path, you lose your way. This is also another dangerous aspect of this option because as clever as it seems, it is not a smart option at all.

Many people have veered off the designated path because they were avoiding the difficulties that they encountered while on their journey. These people go off course because they are avoiding the mountain in their path and are unknowingly avoiding the growth steps of their existence. Imagine if Michael Jordan avoided the fact he did not make the basketball team and quit basketball altogether or did not work harder to become greater. He would not have ever become the person he is today. Jordan once stated in a magazine that he never let the pain of not making the varsity basketball team go, and this hurt helped him win six NBA championships while eventually becoming the first basketball player to become a billionaire. Do you get it? The pain that Michael experienced at the age of fifteen or sixteen is part of the reason for his success, and this was experienced as an adolescent youth.

Yes, you have to go through the mountain, or in this case, across and over it, to reach the intended destination, which allows you to benefit from the experience. I remember what my mother told me about running from problems as you will eventually run away from yourself. The results are equally the same when a person avoids their problems. Therefore, we should make sure that we do not deviate from the right path, which may be difficult, in search of easier ways that will lead us away from our target destination. Don't waste your time going around your mountain because if you do, you will definitely miss out on the lesson that is on the mountain.

OPTION 4: YOU CAN CLIMB UP THE MOUNTAIN!

So life is going well or as good as it gets. Everything is going in the right direction. It is like you cannot make any mistakes, or it will be the complete opposite scenario, being that everything is not going right and life is not going well. Everything gets worse as the days go by. Out of nowhere, you are placed at the bottom of a mountain, and this structure represents one of the biggest obstacles of your life. Yes, you can run away, complain about it, or avoid the mountain, but this time, you look directly at the obstacle and climb it.

Yes, you can do it, and in fact, this is the best option! This option should be the only option that you ever consider in life. Aggressively confronting your mountains and scaling each one of them, one by one, is the obvious correct answer to successfully conquering life's mountains. This is both literally and figuratively the only way to truly *get over* your problems. I recently became attached to a quote that states, "The best view comes after the hardest climb," which connects the idea of the hard journey of life to the benefits of overcoming the struggle. Many benefits can be derived from climbing mountains besides successfully crossing over to the other side.

Primarily, climbing a mountain strengthens you. The mountain has the ability to add strength, both physically and mentally. The more a person climbs, the stronger they become. The more a person endures while climbing, the tougher they become. My friend, Benjamin, became stronger because of his tough experiences throughout his life. This new addition of strength is unavoidable. This experience is similar to working out. The more we exercise our bodies, the more our bodies adapt to the exercises by adding more muscle fibers. This addition accounts for and covers the extra strain that is taking place inside the body. In essence, this leads to more bulk, more growth, and generally, more strength to carry on with more exercise. This is proven science.

In the same way, facing problems in life and tackling them benefits our bodies and, most importantly, our minds. We get stronger physically and mentally when we tackle our problems. What doesn't kill us makes us stronger. When we become physically and mentally stronger, we find out that the problem becomes easier and more minuscule because we have elevated ourselves above the level of the problem. We have gotten stronger than the problem. Hence, we tend to overcome it easier than we thought. Even though we might encounter a lot of pain and discouragement, these experiences should not deter or influence us to take our eyes off the goals and the benefits that are available during the entire process while facing our problems.

We have everything to gain and nothing to lose when we confront our mountains. Facing and overcoming your traumas is one of the only ways to experience success. Weird statement, huh? Close your eyes and think about all of the success stories that were created out of pain and misery. _____ (Insert name) experienced neglect, rape, abuse, drug use, or _____ (insert problem) throughout their childhood/life and is now one of the most successful people on earth. Former college football player and currently one of the top motivational speakers, Inquoris "Inky" Johnson, faced an extremely steep and tall mountain as a top 30 NFL recruit.

During his last year in college, his right arm was left paralyzed after an on-field collision. He was from extreme poverty, and he needed football to save his situation. This injury closed the door on his NFL dreams. Instead of being hurt, Inky faced and walked up the mountain. He is now a top motivational speaker for schools, community centers, and ceremonies throughout the U.S.

In the long run, tackling the problem or climbing the mountain automatically makes us bigger than the problem or bigger than the mountain, and we find out that we can and will be victorious, contrary to our initial beliefs that these problems or mountains will overwhelm us. It is extremely essential to avoid having a negative mindset toward your problem and make sure that you are taking that initial positive *step* towards solving your problem. Remember, the only way to make a positive step forward is by taking a positive step forward. When we do this, the odds are in our favor to succeed.

So how does a person actually climb their mountain? How do we make sure that we are ready to face our obstacles and overcome them? Is there a procedure for tackling the challenges in life? What am I doing wrong when I face the challenges in life because they always beat me? These are some of the questions that drive us crazy on a daily basis, and most of the time, we find it difficult suffering and searching for the answers to them. After going over the available options while at the bottom of a mountain, next, we will go over the details of how to go about climbing mountains to give us a more elaborate understanding of the process involved in overcoming our obstacles.

Chapter Three

CLIMBING THE MOUNTAIN

"Every problem is a gift – without problems we would not grow." –**Anthony Robbins**

Climbing the mountain successfully involves four intricate processes that must be implemented and not just some spur of the moment kind of push. You don't just wake up one hot sunny day and walk up to some random mountain—no ropes, no water reserves, heck, no climbing shoes or gear—and attempt to climb it because you've always felt like hiking. Imagine being at the bottom of an actual mountain in your pajamas and flip-flops trying to scale it. I don't even want to picture how that will turn out, but I know the media would love to cover the story of the body of the pajama-ed person that everyone walks over each year and takes awesome selfies with.

Steps can be taken to ensure that you climb up the mountain in the right way, and steps can also be taken to properly scale the mountains of life.

We will discuss the four steps as follows:

STEP ONE - IDENTIFYING THE PROBLEM

The first step is identifying the actual problem. This step can get pretty confusing as many tend to misidentify their problems, which lead to additional strenuous issues. If you fail to identify the exact problem or if you misidentify the problem, you run the risk of slowing the process and starting off on the wrong foot, which leads to wasting valuable time, energy, and resources all for the wrong reasons. This can cause extreme frustration and may discourage an individual from giving their best effort when they are tackling future challenges as the illusion appears that the results are always the same.

It is like the unfortunate situations that occur in hospitals when a disease is misdiagnosed and mistaken for another, either due to negligence or to a faulty process or machinery. As a result, the actual disease that requires treatment ends up not being treated properly. Unfortunately, the result of this treatment process is not too positive and almost always leads to even more problems. Identifying the exact problem is key to solving it. Another example is when an individual experiences hard times in life. They could easily be tempted to misidentify the problem being experienced as bad luck while ignoring the underlying factors that are causing their state. Many factors may play into the reason why they may be experiencing hardship or a slew of unlucky events.

You must take responsibility for every situation, and it will make it easier to identify the actual problem. For example, you are running late for work, and while on the route, you are caught by every single stoplight. You curse the stoplights and blame your tardiness on every single stoplight, but if you took a look through the lens of responsibility, you might notice it is actually your fault. Since you were not prepared to be at work on time or to make it to work at your start time, you depended on unpredictable stoplights instead of relying on your calculated self during which you could have left earlier or could have performed some kind of action that would have assisted in avoiding the tardiness. It is important to take control of the things that seem uncontrollable. Most people will complain at each stoplight and arrive at work to continue to complain about their circumstances saying, "I am so unlucky," but is this statement really true? If you show accountability, it will help to identify the overall issue.

This is also the case for someone who has gone through emotional or physical abuse. A victim of a sexual assault, especially if it takes place at an early stage in life, normally causes detrimental developmental consequences to the victim. According to The National Sexual Violence Research Center, many victims struggle with anxiety, depression, intrusive memories, and intimacy difficulties. This trauma can affect the victim anywhere in life, and if one problem is tackled, another will always crop up in its place. These consequences will remain until the underlying problem, which is the early sexual trauma, is addressed. One of the greatest authors and poets of all-time, Maya Angelou, revealed details about her sexual assault in her 1969 autobiography, *I Know Why the Caged Bird Sing*. In this masterpiece, Angelou revealed that she was raped when she was eight years old, and after the man responsible was released from prison, he was murdered, causing her to become mute. This masterful speaker, as we know her, did not speak for nearly five years. She is quoted as taking responsibility for killing the man that abused her because she released his name to the authorities and eventually to the media. When this happened, Maya Angelou's name was

Marguerite Annie Johnson. When she finally climbed the mountains that were placed before her, she overcame her past. After getting married and starting her career, she then changed her name to what we now know her as. She climbed her mountains and became the great Maya Angelou!

Maya Angelou's voice will never be forgotten, and once she identified the problem, she could begin to ascend the mountains of life. Angelou once stated, "There is no agony like bearing an untold story inside you." If no action is taken on the root of the issue, there will not be a definitive fix to the additional weeds that keep cropping up. However, recovery is possible, especially if the individual seeks the appropriate help like therapy, treatment, or sometimes just open dialogue with someone who cares. All of these options could be beneficial. Therefore, care should be taken in understanding the root cause of the problem.

This first step is significant to getting started on the right track, and like a third grader solving a word problem in math class, understanding the problem is the first step to solving it. When we identify the root cause of the problem, only then can we make a productive effort in tackling it and eventually overcoming it.

STEP TWO - DEVELOPING A POSITIVE MINDSET

After identifying the problem, how we actually think or feel about the issue before us is extremely important. Honestly, how do you really feel about tackling this problem? Do you feel that it is something beyond your control? Do you feel that this issue is too overwhelming? Do you feel that this mountain is something you cannot overcome or that it is too big of an issue that you cannot climb? How convinced are you that you can tackle this problem? Have you said fake words to yourself like, can't, impossible, and won't?

You see, walking up to the mountain and facing it is one thing, but truthfully believing that you can overcome it is another. American singer, songwriter, actor, author, poet, and activist, Willie Nelson, once said, "Once you replace negative thoughts with positive ones, you'll start having positive results." Top motivational speaker, Mike Adams, also states, "Each person has the motivation and the drive to become self-disciplined if they put their minds to it and the time and effort that will be required for success." It is essential to develop a positive mindset about the problem you are facing and put your mind to use solving it. You can do this by seeing the obstacle, not as a problem, but as a step towards something much greater. You must change the way that you look at problems. Maya Angelou experienced extreme hardships that propelled her to becoming a phenomenal woman. Her journey has inspired and influenced so many others to becoming and believing that they too are phenomenal despite their circumstances.

    Even gold is purified by passing through fire and going through the melting process, and there is a popular saying that pressure creates diamonds and fire refines gold. This saying can be applied to your situation. See obstacles as the pressure to your diamond and the fire to your gold. Remember that there is no known natural substance that can destroy gold, so your chances of success are golden. Just know that you will be successful after you experience your melting process.

    Your problems can be further viewed as processes that you must pass through to come out bigger, better, and stronger. Make up your mind and convince yourself that you can overcome any situation that you encounter, and you will have taken another vital step toward approaching your mountain. There is great power in positive thinking and developing a positive mindset. It is up to you to fully harness that power.

    A positive mindset is incredibly beneficial. It will give you the drive you need each day to wake up and keep pushing forward in the face of adversity. It will propel you forward when every other thing in life pulls you backwards. One of the great minds, Zig Ziglar, stated, "Positive thinking will let you do everything better than negative thinking will," and that is a subtle way to think about the power of positive thinking. Why think negatively when it has the least amount of rewards? When you develop a positive mindset, you let go of all the negativity in your life that might be a cog in your wheel of progress. This may include letting go of people, especially if they are not on the same journey towards greatness as you, and this even applies to friends and/or family that you may have known your entire life.

If there are people in your life that only provide negativity and slow down the process of climbing your mountains, you must leave them behind on the mountainside, or their negativity will weigh you down, causing you to share their same fate. A positive mindset will make you forgive whatever it was that brought pain in the past and help you move forward. It will not only make you stronger, but it also makes those around you stronger. It will help you see life from a primarily positive point of view, and when you get to this stage, you have already made significant progress towards overcoming your mountain.

STEP THREE - TAKE THE RIGHT STEPS TOWARDS ADDRESSING THE PROBLEM

Having convinced yourself that the mountain, no matter how insurmountable it may seem, is something that you can successfully scale, you can now move forward. It is essential to take the right steps to help you achieve your ultimate goal of conquering the mountain before you. Preparing yourself for the challenges ahead is extremely important to your progress up the mountain. After preparing yourself mentally by developing a positive mindset, the next steps are to physically prepare yourself for the quest ahead.

Physical preparation is a vital part of the process, and you should do everything to avoid being like the pajamas-clad-spur-of-the-moment hiker that shows up at the bottom of the mountain and missing the plans to overcome the treacherous conditions. We all know misfortune is sure to come for this unprepared hiker. However, misfortune does not have to come for you. So, in order to be successful, it is crucial to have the necessary measures and plan in place. This is the third vital step to climbing the mountain, and it is an all-important one. If you don't plan ahead when facing your problems, you are undoubtedly planning to fail. Identifying the problem and having a positive mindset will not be enough, especially if you don't figure out how to physically equip yourself before attempting to handle your problems.

Taking the necessary steps can come in various ways such as:

1. **Seeking treatment even if the problem is not a highly psychological or traumatic one.**
2. **Putting measures in place to help curtail bad habits after identifying them.**
3. **Staying away from people that negatively influence you and creating deeper connections to people that could possibly motivate and help you achieve your goals whether short- or long-term.**

When the necessary steps have been taken, you are undoubtedly putting yourself through the process of climbing mountains, and ultimately, this process of seeking a greater you will remove any distractions that will otherwise cause a loss of focus.

When you take the necessary steps, like seeking treatment and choosing the right social circle, you are automatically adding personal benefits by getting yourself ready for the challenges ahead. You may attract the right connections that help foster your success and provide some added motivation that assists with overcoming your mountain. Most of the time, people can attract others who share the same or similar problems that they have. Therefore, you have company on the journey to overcoming your mountain, and just as in the real sense of it, hiking is much more enjoyable when done in groups that positively motivate each other.

The process of overcoming obstacles results in being one that you can enjoy due to the support and motivation that you are gifted by taking the right steps. Even when your mountain is so unique that you do not meet support groups with the exact similar problem (*Chances are you will likely meet people with similar problems anyway*.), you end up being the only one climbing your mountain, and you will still scale it successfully and come out on top. This success happens because you have put in the necessary measures ensuring your progress.

STEP FOUR - CLIMB THE MOUNTAIN

With the problem identified, a positive mindset developed, and a specific plan put in place, there isn't much preventing your successful journey up and over your mountain. Your next steps are simple. Climb your mountain!

As you start to climb your mountain, you will notice a lot of negative and discouraging changes. The changes are similar to someone who does not normally workout, and as they begin to exercise, if they go beyond their must-stop point, their muscles will become strained, causing some serious body pains. For example, if lifting weights for the first time in a long time, the arms will hurt at the slightest move, and this pain is severe enough to put upcoming workout plans in jeopardy. It is important to understand that pain is a natural part of the process. If you stop exercising after the first sign of pain, why start in the first place? Pain tolerance is a prerequisite to exercise. This pain is understood, expected, and respected. It is important to keep this same thinking in mind when trying to overcome your mountain.

It is possible that while on your journey you may experience pain, disappointment, and discouragement as temptation may even try to persuade you to give up along the way, but it is important to stay the course by keeping your eyes on the prize and maintaining your momentum. You must keep taking small aggressive steps. Great philosopher, Socrates, once declared to people, "Be as you wish to seem." So, be exceptional and be resilient. Rest assured that you have all that you need to overcome the mountain that threatens you and since you diligently prepared for it, expect success. After utilizing all of the necessary steps to overcoming your problem, you will have earned the opportunity to enjoy the best view yet.

My childhood friend, Ben, started the process of overcoming his problems by making an extremely uncomfortable but necessary decision. Ben first identified his problem, which he realized all rooted from a traumatic childhood filled with both physical and emotional abuse. He developed a positive mindset after gaining strength by realizing that his future is stronger because of this trauma-filled past, and he began to notice that due to this thinking, he was starting to make tremendous progress. Ben then took the necessary step of seeking treatment to assist in overcoming this psychological problem.

Seeking help is not a bad or shameful action as it is not related to having a mental illness in any way. *Everyone experiences trauma in life, but our response to these situations decide our future mental, emotional, societal, and personal development.* Most of the time, we are unaware that we have been impacted by traumas. Our early trauma can decide how we unconsciously respond to our surroundings in the future. I have come in contact with many individuals that despite being very much past adulthood, they still blame their parents or events from childhood for their current situations in life, just as Ben did.

As an adult, it is up to the individual to be in complete control of their happiness as parents are not in any way responsible for this. Remember that you are responsible for you. Therapy can assist in the healing and closure process that you may not be able to reach alone. We are all humans, and vulnerability is a part of human nature. Ben felt overwhelmed, and initially, he was afraid to seek therapy because of his ill-conceived opinions about psychology and about himself. Never be intimidated when you are taking the steps that are necessary to move forward. Seek the appropriate help anytime that you feel like something is or about to overwhelm you.

During Ben's therapy, he was able to dig down deep inside of himself to find and understand that *a bad or ugly beginning does not automatically translate to a terrible ending.* He began to understand that he could use the anger and pain from these bad experiences as the fuel he needed to push out positive reactions, which led Ben successfully to overcoming his problems at hand. He first learned to forgive himself as this action was the most essential part of his early process. This is detailed as *forgiveness therapy* as he then learned to forgive others, like his father's killer and his uncle, and this brought about an immense relief that Ben could never have imagined. This process does not in any way mean forgetting or condoning the experienced bad behavior but, instead, letting go of the leftover resentment and hate. After this experience, Ben became liberated. By letting go of his past, changing his perspective, and ultimately setting himself free, Ben overcame his first mountain. Ironically, this first mountain was one which Benjamin had subconsciously imposed on himself as he had no idea it even existed. Having done this, Ben could focus on the next mountain of making his negative life positive and worthwhile. After years of having bad reactions, gaining control of his reactions ended up being a very simple process for him in general.

At times, this process of facing your mountain will appear to be overcomplicated. This mountain journey can and will seem impossible. This is one of the main reasons why the average person runs away from each mountain they encounter. But once you begin to confront them, each mountain at its base or the problems in life from their root, you will realize that the *process* is a natural procedure that the mind and body is naturally ready for. The stories about Benjamin, Michael Jordan, Maya Angelou, and Samantha are examples of how the mountains from the past can hold you back, but when you eventually face and climb the mountains in your life, only then can you get to the top and successfully overcome your problems, allowing yourself the ability to continue on life's journey.

Chapter Four

LOOKING BACK: R & C (REFLECT & CELEBRATE)

"When nobody else compliments you, then compliment yourself. It's not up to other people to keep you encouraged. It's up to you. Encouragement should come from the inside." – **Joel Osteen**

Now that you have successfully overcome the first part of your obstacle, you should feel amazing even if the result of your climb did not go exactly as planned. The most important point to understand is that you have finally scaled your mountain, and boy, the view is amazing! You have achieved part of your set goals, and you have finally gotten one-up on your problems. Congratulations! So, what is the next thing you need to do? This phase has to be one of the most important steps of the mountain process. This step is another aspect of life that most people almost always get wrong. Some people are in so much of a hurry after overcoming their obstacles that they miss the subtle necessities that are needed for self-preservation, self-care, and self-encouragement. After successfully climbing up their mountains, most individuals move so fast down to the other side of the mountain that they miss the incredible event that has just taken place. Many rush to get over their problems in order to quickly forget about them. They race to the finish line. While this can be understandable, it is highly discouraged.

It is extremely important to learn the necessary lessons at this point. Do not be in such a rush that you clamber down the mountain. No, you should stop to take a breather! Stop, think, and reflect at this point of your journey. Rest, take a look around you, look back, and appreciate the moment. Enjoy the beautiful view that the top of the mountain and treacherous journey has afforded you. Remember that you prepared for this and worked hard to get here, so why not revel in it, even if for just a moment?

This metaphorical moment translates to appreciating the things that you have overcome in life. If you survived a divorce, this is where you swim in success. If you are a foster child and are still breathing and progressing through life, swim in your success. If you have overcome the odds that life has thrown your way, swim in success. This is your opportunity to find value in the life experiences that often get taken for granted. Many of my students do not realize that they are already walking samples of success because they have survived many distressing circumstances but are still able to be in a place of massive opportunity. If positive perspective is taken into account, they would cheer their existence. They would realize their accomplishments, like surviving childhood rape, abuse, neglect, poverty, or life in general. English Romantic poet, William Wadsworth, once famously exclaimed, "Rest and be thankful." It is important to perform both actions as this is maybe one of the only opportunities that you have for thought and reflection, so use it.

It is important to celebrate yourself as you progress along your journey because it is no one else's responsibility to keep your head above water. Keeping *you* happy is a *you* thing, and this should be something that *you* keep number one on your list of priorities. In order to help others, you must first help yourself. It is not the responsibility of any other living person in existence to keep you happy and sane. Don't expect a crowd to be waiting for you at the top of the mountain, singing adulations and applauding your efforts and achievements. Most of the time in life, people won't recognize your true greatness, so it is your number one job to recognize yourself. Remember that you have to be your own favorite cheerleader and you are expected to be an extraordinary one because you owe it to yourself. So go on and applaud yourself. Good job, self! *Celebrate* what you have overcome.

This is the current problem with social media and the depression that results once a person goes unnoticed by others. In the age of social media and technology, many depend on the opinions of others. The opinion of others is just that - opinions. You have to be your first friend. There is a need for too much outside adulation and praise when, as stated before, that it is no one's responsibility to keep you happy but yourself. This is something that needs consistent work and attention.

There is a famous African anecdote, most notably detailed in the masterpiece novel, *Things Fall Apart*, by legendary writer, Chinua Achebe, that tells a story about a lizard that loses its balance, falls from the top of a remarkably and amazingly tall Iroko tree, and lands on his feet unharmed. Once on the ground, the lizard looks around and notices there is no one present to praise it, so it turns around, nods its head, and praises itself. Wow, what a lizard! Do you need an audience present to celebrate your accomplishments? Does greatness require a witness to be considered greatness?

You should be like the lizard that fell from the tree. Take your opportunity to reflect on what you overcame. Reflection and celebration are some of the most important steps of this process because it assists us in fully getting over each of the mountains in our lives. This is your opportunity to celebrate your successes so far. To finally give yourself credit for your experiences and celebrating that part of your problem is now behind you. When at the top of the mountain, you need to make it a habit to always look back and reflect on each lesson you have learned or what you should have learned while on the journey and celebrate your location because one of your problems is now in your rear view mirror. Danish philosopher and author, Soren Kierkegaard, once voiced, "Life can only be understood backwards; but it must be lived forward." It is important to take breaks for reflection as this is one of the only opportunities you have to learn the necessary lessons of life's journey.

Remember to keep in mind that the obstacles we encounter all have a larger purpose and they are not in our lives for the sake of being a nuisance during the process to becoming successful. **You must deeply reflect on each and every one of the lessons, reflect on the cause or causes of the obstacles truly recognizing the reasons why they were there in the first place, reflect on the methods of how you prevailed over them, and reflect on how overcoming them have made you better.** There is always a lesson to be learned at each stage of your journey over the mountain. You must be patient while reflecting so you do not to miss out on anything. It is very important not to take your experiences for granted.

When you think about the problems you encountered while climbing your mountain and reflect on how you overcame them, your self-esteem will automatically receive a boost. You will and should feel very proud of yourself, and this in itself is a vital step and a motivating factor that will lend a huge hand in helping you scale down the other side of your mountain.

Even if there may be problems that resulted in no solution or issues that ended up not receiving the greatest resolutions, you can still move past those problems but only through self-evaluation and critical analysis. You can celebrate your growth as you stand at the top of your mountains. When you are finally able to revel on your successes, you will then have the ability and the mental fortitude to reflect on your failures and the reasons you did not achieve success in the first place.

You have to take charge of your emotions and dictate for yourself how you should feel. Sometimes we criticize ourselves too much, searching for imperfections more than we examine ourselves searching to commemorate our many achievements. One of those achievements can simply be breathing. Oftentimes, making it out of situations alive is a feat in itself. I have taught so many students who have been drowning in traumatic situations their entire lives. The fact that these students even attend school with an opportunity in front of them, whether small or large, is an achievement in itself. This is very hard to see when you are climbing and have been climbing for so long.

As you ascend your mountain, you can only see the current chaos that is directly in front of you. So when you finally reach the top of your climb, look back to reflect on your journey in celebration and evaluation. Do not wait for validation from other people as the applauding, whistling, and happy cheers may never come. Social media increases depression and loneliness because of our dependence on another individual's approval when most of the time, just like the African lizard, we are great on our own and do not need others to recognize our greatness. Yes, it is true that you should definitely treat others as you want them to treat you, but if you do not have value for yourself, others will treat you terribly. No one will ever treat you how you should treat yourself. Others either have just finished scaling their own mountains and might also be waiting for validation and applause, or they don't care enough to provide you encouragement. However, you should not let this neglect of greatness negatively affect your own self-esteem. You should always be your own number one fan! You should give yourself one million likes and feel good about it. Self-management of your self-esteem is vital. It is essential to control all that you can control when it comes to your self-esteem, and this is why a reflective analysis of your experiences is extremely necessary.

My former student, Sam, and old friend, Ben, initially never celebrated themselves due to the fact that they never reflected on their accomplishments. They never realized that regardless of their circumstances, they were making tremendous strides. Sam was already in high school when we first met. This meant that she was in the ninth grade with an opportunity to continue her journey further, which in itself is a great accomplishment for anyone, especially someone who has gone through the battles that she had. She was not without opportunity, but what's an opportunity when you don't see, acknowledge, and/or even recognize it as such?

Sam went on to become an honors student throughout the rest of high school, and this happened because she realized that she was the main reason for her own survival. She realized her own strengths and her minimal amount of weaknesses that was a factor of her past actions and disposition. She realized that all the experiences in her life were there for a purpose. She figured out that these experiences were present to teach her lessons and prepare her for the future. Sam took all of her negative experiences and turned them into the fire for her inner gold. She overcame hopelessness and is now doing quite well, both socially and academically. After each successful semester, Sam would analyze herself and enjoy her successes. She became proud of her achievements, and this invariably became a ritual that would spur her on for the challenges of the upcoming semester. After she analyzed herself each time, she would often joke and laugh about her past experiences. She would say to herself as she recorded a recurring reminder message on her phone, "You are the only one responsible for making yourself feel good and to smile. No one can take the blame for you not giving yourself credit when it is due because you deserve it." She found the importance of saying affirmations in order to rebuild herself through the mountain process.

Ben also did not have any idea that he had made so many accomplishments in life, especially based on his background in gangs and upbringing in chaos. This is because at the time he never looked back when he got to the top of his mountains. Ben's father was murdered, and he just kept moving. He was abused, and he just kept moving. Ben continued this same process until he unknowingly started following a formula. His formula was simple as he believed bad things always happened because they were supposed to, so he just let them happen and kept moving. After Ben changed things around, he noticed how fortunate he was after surviving so much. In the past, he failed to notice his tremendous progress to becoming virtually indestructible. I mean, after his experiences in life, what more could he not handle? He has been through everything. When Ben finally recognized his story and eventually his accomplishments, he could celebrate his freedom and realize that the future was his for the taking.

It is tremendously important to celebrate your successes and immediately reflect once you get past your problem. Salute the steps that you have made on your journey. The stories of Ben, Sam, Jordan, Angelou, and even the African lizard are not here to motivate you, but they are also meant to serve as practical guides that you can relate to. These stories are examples of individuals climbing and overcoming their mountains, showing that anything can be achieved when the right steps are taken despite living and experiencing traumatic circumstances.

Chapter Five

CLIMBING DOWN & MOVING ON

"The foolish man lies awake all night long thinking of his many problems; when the morning comes he is worn out and his trouble is just as it was." – **Norse Proverb**

Now you have taken some time to reflect, think, and react while you are on top of the mountain and have given yourself that well-deserved pat on the back. You have rejoiced in your successes and have reviewed the reasons for your failures and/or mistakes along the way. You have looked back on what you have overcome. Alas, it's time to move on to the next phase, and that is climbing down the other side. This is usually the tricky part of the process. You must be a bit exhausted by your efforts so far in getting to the top of the mountain, but you have to persevere by climbing down the other side towards the finish line. To achieve completion, you have to first make sure not to spend too much time at the top of the mountain thinking and reflecting about your journey. Just as not taking the necessary time to appreciate your journey is risky, taking too much time reflecting on the journey or getting too intoxicated by the euphoria at having reached the top of the mountain is equally dangerous. *You cannot move forward until you stop looking back, and it is impossible to stay focused on the dreams that are in front of you if you cannot get over what is behind you.*

How does this translate to life problems? When you have significantly overcome the major part of a problem and have taken the time to appreciate yourself for your efforts, be wary not to get carried away by the joy of getting to this stage. Always bear in mind that the last part of your journey still remains, and that is climbing down to the other side. You cannot say that you have fully overcome an obstacle just by getting to the top of it. You must get over it, and it is as simple as it sounds. To fully prevail over a problem, one must completely get over their problem. So, while you are lauding yourself for the incredible achievement of getting to the top of the mountain, know that the finish line is waiting for you at the foot of the mountain on the other side.

Many believe that starting is the hardest part of any process, but finishing is actually the most difficult part of almost anything. Great philosopher and father of Western education, Plato, once stated, "A good start is half the battle." As I reiterated this idea earlier in the book, there is another famous quote that states, "Starting is difficult, finishing is much harder." Finishing any task takes much more dedication and hard work than beginning a task. This idea can be seen in action usually after you have taken a trip. The commute back usually seems the longest. If you have ever observed or participated in marathon running, the final leg of the race is the most difficult. The participants usually start off running full of energy and excitement. However, as the race progresses and the minutes turn into hours, their strength begins to wane, and they gradually slow down as they near the finish. While spectating Chicago's 26-mile marathon, I have seen individuals give up mid-trip, and I have witnessed injuries plague runners as they near the finish line. It takes a lot of sustained effort, resilience, and endurance to finish one of these races. The same way of thinking can be applied when dealing with the problems in life. Setting up for the finish can be the hardest part of overcoming life's mountains. Most people falsely believe that starting is the most difficult part of a task, but taking the final steps are often part of life's most daunting tasks. It takes a lot of sustained effort, resilience, and endurance to finish and close out life's problems. So make sure to finish whatever you start.

As you are celebrating yourself and descending into deep reflection, you are allowed the opportunity to think about all the other minor problems that you have encountered while on your way to overcoming your ultimate issue. You now know how important it is to think about the issues that you overcame in addition to the problems that you failed to find a great solution for. While you are doing this, you should make sure not to waste too much time looking back on all the things that you have experienced, good or bad, as they are now a part of the past. The only thing that mattered when you were on top of the mountain was making sure that you learned the lessons that each of the difficulties presented while you were on the journey to overcoming your problems. While on the way down or past your problem, you must make sure to take in, or absorb, each lesson and move on. Mulling over all the problems that you overcame over and over and over again will prevent you from successfully climbing down the mountain as you are yet to fully let go of your past. Letting go of the past can be one of the hardest steps of the mountain process.

For maximum progress, both Sam and Ben were obligated to climb down their mountains but, most importantly, move on from their past issues. They both realized they must let go of their pasts in order to move forward. It is crucial to let go of the things that anchor you down, and it is essential to learn from your experiences. Remember, letting go of things can also include people.

Growing up, Sam suffered abuse and neglect. She initially viewed these experiences as terrible and traumatic events. These events aided in breaking her as a person, but when she began using the process, she could view these events as the boost she needed to become a person of strength, understanding, and resilience. Initially, Sam was ashamed of her experiences until she changed her perspective and found the strength in the same exact experiences that were giving her grief. Perspective is what the brain sees, and having a good mind view is essential to success. If you constantly beat yourself up about the things that are and were out of your control, how will you ever progress?

SKILL ONE: THE TALK-POSITIVE SELF-AWARENESS

One of the most essential skills necessary in successfully completing the mountain process is self-motivation. You must learn how to positively *talk* to yourself and then wholeheartedly *listen* to your inner responses. You must learn to talk yourself through the difficult times and through any weak moments that you may experience. Talk yourself through the pain. Tell yourself to always make it to the finish line while keeping in mind that there are mandatory benefits waiting for you at the bottom of the mountain. This self-conversation must be filled with inspiration and positivity. Remember, you are your own cheerleader, so negativity is not allowed in this conversation.

There is power in spoken words, so your statements will affect your belief system and success rate in life. Make sure that your words do so positively. For example, there is no such thing as trying. The word, try, is a fake word. Just hear me out. The synonyms of the word try are to make an attempt, give it one's best shot, and undertake, to name a few. The synonym of all of the words or phrases that I have provided point right back to the word, DO. The word, try, prepares an individual to accept failure, so it has no use. Always say, "I will (do)," and you are guaranteed to make achievements. Use statements of power when you speak with yourself.

Initially, when my friend, Benjamin, talked to himself, he predicted and planned his own troubles. He subconsciously planned his troubles because his mind and resulting actions were so negative. He told himself that he was nothing and that he was not headed for a successful future. Ben based his future on his past because he couldn't let go of his past. He only looked back at the things that had gone wrong and never looked forward at the things that could go right. Life gave Ben exactly what he planned for. He planned for nothing and received exactly that. He was ultimately successful in planning for his failures, and his actions assured his direction on this planned path.

As you can see, Ben was extraordinary in poor planning, but after his transformation, Benjamin predicted and planned his successes. Self-management and self-motivation became Ben's success assets. Ben told himself that because of his past, he must be successful. He used his past as fuel to power him down the mountains of his life. He transformed his pain into strength. His hurt was transformed into resilience and his mental misery into memories. Thus, he could overcome the traumas of his past.

SKILL TWO: RPP – POSITIVE THINKING ROUTINE

The second skill necessary in successfully completing the mountain process is **Relentless Positive Perception**. This is much like one of the steps we earlier discussed in Chapter 3, which is used in overcoming the root of the problem when handling mountains from the past. To complete any difficult task, it is important to keep the mind in check. When you are completing rigorous challenges, your mind will be overly susceptible to negative thinking, so it is important to create a positive thinking routine.

When faced with a seemingly enormous task, negative thinking makes it easier to fail. It is important to not think about these tasks or problems as enormous burdens. *You should simply focus on finishing the task at hand by taking small aggressive steps. If you have a task to complete, never passively watch the task. Just get to work and complete it.* Keep your mind off of the finish line. Keep your mind off of the bottom of the mountain. If you are working at your top potential, you will do well at your finish. Your success will come because you diligently prepared for all of this before deciding to climb your mountain.

Never complain about the path while you are on it as you will make the journey a worse experience and might miss your necessary lessons. Complaining also interferes with succeeding, and you will only waste valuable time and energy that you could have put into finishing the task at hand and ultimately helping you to the finish line. Running into obstacles are inevitable, so overcoming negativity in your mind is the best way to treat yourself.

When I met Samantha, she complained about her life. She complained about her past as she absorbed the experiences and used them as anchors. After I began mentoring her and explaining the benefits of **Relentless Positive Perception**, she started to apply the tenets and to view her circumstances differently. She began to realize that she was lucky to experience her circumstances. She took pride in her unexpected life encounters and worked so much harder to accomplish her life goals. This paid huge dividends as she succeeded in turning her negatives into positives and getting her life back on track. That is the power of **Relentless Positive Perception.**

SKILL THREE: THE APPLICATION – PLANNING POINTS

The third and final most important skill necessary in successfully climbing down the mountain is the ability to use experiences as planning points. Remember those lessons that you learned when you paused on top of the mountain to look back? Remember how those experiences were necessary in teaching valuable lessons? Now is the time to apply those lessons.

Both Ben and Sam experienced pain that was caused by chaotic childhoods. Ben's father was shot and killed when he was just five years old. He was abused by his uncle. He committed a crime and was taken into juvenile custody. Sam also had a difficult life. She faced so many obstacles. Sam lived with foster parents after being abused by a close family member for years. This pain was used to keep her down and could have led her to ruin. But both Sam and Ben possessed the ability to plan with pain, and they successfully used their experiences to get to better points in life. They also used their pain and experiences as guides towards writing better conclusions to their stories.

The bad experiences that are encountered in life can be used as planning points. For example, I myself am a child of divorced parents, but instead of being pained and influenced by that experience, I used it as a driving force and a point of reference. I used it as a lesson and a pointer as to what to avoid when I became a husband and father. Now my daughter celebrates a happily married mother and father who provide her a stable home. I also made sure that based on some of my painful and dangerous experiences while growing up in Chicago that my daughter would never experience the same things I experienced. My pain acted as a bookmark for my future planning, and overall, that mindset has helped me significantly in achieving each and every one of my goals. Most of my chaotic childhood experiences were just that, and those experiences helped me to become me. I appreciate every moment.

As you successfully climb your mountains, learn to use the experiences and lessons as a guide on your way down. This means that when you have overcome the significant part of the problem and as you are strutting toward the finish line, use your experience and what you have learned so far to guide you towards making a grand finish. Avoid those things that threatened to derail you on your journey up the mountain and watch out for the inevitable problems that you will encounter on the way down. The final stages are usually the trickiest and most treacherous. The final leg of the journey should be navigated with more experience, which you have successfully garnered during the now completed parts of the mountain.

Media powerhouse and massive mountain climber, Oprah Winfrey, beautifully advises society to, "Turn your wounds into wisdom." Associate professor of American Studies at Brown University, Robert Gary Lee, also proclaims, "Wisdom is nothing more than healed pain." Each interaction and experience on your journey through life teaches something. Even though you may be wounded, you are becoming smarter. Even though you may be in pain, once the pain is healed, you automatically will be wiser and stronger. You have spent valuable time and energy ascending to the peak, so now it is time to finish by using the experience and lessons learned from your journey. Success is waiting. . .

Chapter Six

THE BOTTOM OF THE MOUNTAIN

"No matter how full the river, it still wants to grow."
– **Congolese Proverb**

You have finally come to the end of your mountain journey, having finished your mountain process. You are at the bottom of your mountain. You have crossed over to the other side, and it feels wonderful. But you also feel incredibly exhausted. You feel winded and hurt, and you rightly should. I mean, look at all of what you have overcome. Experience cannot be taught. It must be lived, and you now know this. Look at all the experience that you have gained on this journey. Look at all the lessons that you have learned from this experience. You feel proud of yourself, but mentally you are sore from your climb and eventual descent. You find the closest corner and crumble in a heap, trying to regain your strength and wondering if dealing with the problem was really worth it.

PAIN MANAGEMENT

The pain that you are experiencing is extremely necessary. It is commonly said in the world of exercise that "no pain is equal to no gain." In the same way, you should use your pain as an indicator of getting better. You must perceive the pain as a cleansing tool and use it as a weapon of refinement. Know that the pain you are feeling is there to make you whole again. The pain exists to make you stronger and even more prepared for the journey ahead as you heal. The pain is there as a constant reminder that overcoming your obstacles and climbing your mountain is never an easy task. This idea is even understood by hikers, bicyclists, and adventurists that participate in death-defying treks for fun and leisure. Pain is a part of the process, and it is okay to experience pain as we struggle to overcome the difficult situations that life has given us. There is a popular belief that success directly correlates to the amount of pain that you feel and to the amount of effort that you have put in. What does this mean? This simply implies that the more pain you feel in addition to the more effort you put in equals the more success you achieve.

Many times, people get discouraged whenever they experience pain in the course of their journey. They forget that nothing good comes easy. Life, as earlier stated, is a journey riddled with obstacles. Some of the obstacles will be easy to overcome, and others will be so grueling, punishing, and demanding that they will be extremely difficult and impossible to conquer. Obstacles, life's impediments, or problems wouldn't be called these things if they were invented to be easy to bypass. Therefore, you should see your pain as an indication that you are in the progress of overcoming your obstacles. Let this pain be your fuel. Let it be your drive to not feel defeated. You wouldn't feel pain or be exhausted if you hadn't summoned up the courage in the first place to face your problems head-on. Convince yourself that this pain you are feeling only exists because you have rightly put in enough effort to overcome the obstacles in life.

Notable actress and activist, Angelina Jolie, once said, "Without pain, there would be no suffering, without suffering we would never learn from our mistakes." She went on to state, "To make it right, pain and suffering is the key to all windows, without it, there is no way of life." This way of thinking is very applicable to every situation in life. Pain, due to progress, should never be viewed as a bad thing. Rather, it should be anticipated and appreciated. Pain represents a significant part of the climbing process, and it is not possible to successfully experience the mountain process without feeling pain.

Pain is a vital part of your journey, so embrace it. Look forward to it because whenever you feel it, you are on the right track. This way of thinking can be applied to anything from relationship management to grades in school to health. You should develop a mindset that if you don't feel pain when on your journey to overcome the mountains in your life, then you are not fully following the mountain process. That mountain then was never really a mountain. Look at it this way. If hiking was that easy and pain-free, what thrill would trekkers gain from successfully scaling new heights time and time again? What motivation would they have to complete a journey if every single person could easily do it? The journey wouldn't have much value anymore as it is something that anybody can easily do.

Many enthusiasts want to scale either one of the two most treacherous mountains in the world. These two mountains are featured on many bucket lists. These individuals are interested in climbing K2 or Mount Everest at least once in their lifetime. If this feat was viewed as being simple and pain-free, it would never make it on anyone's bucket list. Mount Everest is the world's highest mountain, which is why mountaineers view it as an extremely desirable location, but as I earlier detailed, the mountain has an ever-growing body count.

People are motivated by difficulty. These people want to achieve impossible feats that average people find impossible. The world's most successful people have all had similar experiences. Think about the mountains of Steve Jobs, Bill Gates, Albert Einstein, Oprah Winfrey, Michael Jordan, and Maya Angelou and I could name so many more. Connect your pain to these stories and don't let pain and exhaustion pull you down. You get to feel this way because you have successfully overcome a problem in your life. This accomplishment is what most people strive to achieve, and by having achieved it, you should applaud yourself.

You must force yourself to find the positive side of every situation. As stated earlier by Oprah Winfrey, "Turn your wounds into wisdom," and this is a very short but direct piece of advice. It is a very powerful statement, especially looking at Oprah Winfrey's story. She was physically abused, raped, and molested as early as the age of nine by her cousin, uncle, and a family friend. She endured the pain and hurt for several more years before running away from home and experiencing a rough interaction on the streets. She was nearly sent to juvenile incarceration because of her behavior. As this was all happening, Oprah became pregnant and gave birth to a premature boy. She faced problem after problem. She used her package of painful experiences as her main drive and motivation to succeed. According to Winfrey, she does not regret her early struggles and pain, which lasted for most of her adolescent years. Oprah Winfrey's story is a powerful example of someone that has used pain to become wiser and stronger, inside and out.

How does pain make us wiser? How do we turn our wounds and the pain that comes with them into wisdom? We can do this by seeing the pain as a motivational factor and part of the process to achieving our purpose. Even though the pain might discourage you and make it seem like the whole journey over the mountain was a total waste of time, you should always look on the brighter side of things. This is your opportunity to prove your **Relentless Positive Perception**. Yes, you developed the courage to face your mountain, planned well for it, and then successfully scaled it, and now at the bottom on the other side, you feel tired and sore. Well, look on the bright side of things. Your road is now clear, and you can successfully continue on life's journey. There is a whole new plain ahead of you. You would not have seen the flatlands if you didn't rise up and climb your mountain.

Would you rather be back where you were in the beginning, stuck in a rut? Were you better off when you ran away, complained, and avoided your mountain? The answer is a big fat NO! You would have never made progress if you did not make the decision to face and climb over your obstacle. You must climb over obstacles to move forward. Pain is a clear indication that you must have put in diligent effort in moving forward, so instead of wallowing in regret and despair from the pain that results after climbing your mountain, you must look ahead towards the future. Pain is your reward in this scenario. Look at where *pain* has brought you. Appreciate the process and the pain that comes with it. Only then can you fully enjoy the benefits of overcoming your obstacle. Former *Rolling Stones Magazine* editor, Eric Bates, summarizes his ideas on life challenges, "There are no negatives in life, only challenges to overcome that will make you stronger." Life challenges fuel our success and have the ability to make us extraordinary.

Initially, Ben and Sam did not understand this. They failed to realize that pain was part of life's process. They failed to see pain, anguish, and suffering as an indication that they were passing through the mountain process. They both failed to learn what they were supposed to from these tasks, and they did not turn their wounds into wisdom. This left both Ben and Sam in a state of abject self-pity. Even when they successfully scaled the occasional mountains in their lives and made it to the next stage, they still failed to recognize the mountain process and failed take away all the valuable lessons that were available. They saw pain as a negative thing and an impediment that blocked their way to a successful life. They both failed to realize that pain can sometimes be a good sign. They both failed to realize that pain can be an indication of a successful ascent.

After understanding and applying the mountain process, their perception changed tremendously. They both realized that they had been succeeding in life all along without knowing it. They both discovered that they were actually making progress and dispelled their old belief that they could not achieve anything in life. They both recognized that the mountains they'd successfully scaled in the past, even without knowing it, were there to make them stronger and to prepare them for whom they are today. They both recognized pain as part of their healing process, and they learned to embrace it. Both Ben and Sam used their pain and experience as fuel to drive them forward. Now their perception and outlook on life could not be better, and they are both thankful for their experiences and resulted success.

Chapter Seven

EXPECTING MOUNTAINS

"Prepare now for the solutions of tomorrow."
– Congolese Proverb

Now that we have vividly explored ways to successfully tackle a mountain whenever we are faced with one, we must discuss another aspect of life that is equally as important and can help prepare us before we actually address our problems. This preparation strategy is the theory of expecting mountains. It is important that we learn the act of being proactive when dealing with life's situations. It can save us a great deal of time and trouble. Understanding that life is an exciting experience full of mountains, we should then expect the mountains of life even before they come and adequately prepare for them, sort of like having a crystal ball or receiving detailed information from a fortune teller.

As previously pointed out, the mountains of life can come at different points or immediately in succession after each other. There might be a point in our lives when the mountains have taken a break from us, and there are absolutely no mountains in sight. At this moment, everything is working out fine, and plans are falling into place. The tendency is we relax and get complacent. We are tempted to get carried away, and we stop thinking about the possibility of approaching mountains. At this point, we rarely stop to consider what could happen if maybe we lost our job, went through a divorce, lost a loved one, or became sick. We rarely stop to consider how these events would affect our ability to achieve our goals or continue on our journey in life. Being unprepared is not at all the best way to journey through life. It is vital to always prepare ahead of time for any eventuality, especially when things seem rosy. It is vital to prepare ahead of time for the bad times during the good times. Being complacent or too comfortable is a disease, especially in this situation.

What are some ways for us to prepare? This chapter is ponderously packed with tips and strategies that can be followed to be fully or at least somewhat prepared ahead of time for any upcoming mountain or problem in life. The tips are as follows:

I. CARRY OUT EVERYDAY TASKS IN ADVANCE AND COMMIT TO A ROUTINE:

Many of the world's most successful people have a plan of action in which they consistently and successfully complete their daily but difficult tasks each day, and this success happens because they have come up with a strategy to start early and finish early. Most billionaires and millionaires wake up on average around 5:00 a.m. (most earlier) to start their daily routine. You must also devise a way to get the little things done ahead of time, and this should be a regular occurring activity. Consistency is key to this step and is important in completing your tasks. Some of these tasks could include doing your laundry on time, making your bed, cooking in advance, storing the food in the fridge for quick and easy meals, studying or starting homework whenever time permits, cleaning as soon as time provides an opening, and getting appointments out of the way.

Basically, you should use your free time to do any task that you can ahead of its scheduled time. If you work on things early, you will finish early. Complete tasks as soon as possible rather than waiting until the last minute. Great scientist, inventor, and author, Benjamin Franklin, once shared his thoughts about procrastination stating, "You may delay, but time will not, and lost time is never found again." No, time is not recyclable, so once it is gone, it is gone. If time never comes back, why waste it? Why not use time to the best of your abilities and benefit from the way that you utilize it? This is why you must establish a routine beginning early in *your morning*. *Your morning* meaning whatever time that you must wake up (but much earlier than needed) as you may work the night shift and your early morning is in the afternoon. When you commit to routines, you will have far-reaching, long-lasting results. This helps tremendously in your preparation for the mountains of tomorrow.

Write your routine down by recording on your phone using your calendar or typing it out on paper and taping it to your wall. It is important for this routine to be visual, not just a list in your imagination. Eventually as it becomes a habit, you can use your mental paper and pencil to plan your day. Your routine must include the steps that follow or the acronym, **PAMERM**. The awkwardness of the acronym, **PAMERM**, helps me to remember it and keep it a part of my day.

Both **Step I** and **Step IX** will prevent procrastination and ensure efficient time use, especially if you visually plan your schedule.

II. PRACTICE ROUTINE SELF-CARE: PRAY, AFFIRM, MEDITATE, EVALUATE, REFLECT, MOTIVATE (PAMERM)

Much in the same way as you take care of your tasks, you should learn how to take good care of yourself. The clichéd usual suspects are there just as it is important for routine doctor check-ups, regular exercise, and eating healthy, but practicing routine self-care is also significant to your preparation. My morning routine was developed after studying the habits of many of the world's most successful people. This routine has been designed to assist with effectively fueling a person's day. It is extremely important to be in complete control of the way your day begins.

I use the acronym, **PAMERM**, to help remember the order of operations of this step, which acts as my morning routine.

A. PRAY – CLEARING OF THE MIND

This first letter **P for Pray** is important, being that your faith exists in a higher power as this is your opportunity to make and strengthen your connection with your higher power. You can use this opportunity to open your heart, allowing a stronger connection to the universe as a whole. In this situation, you are giving yourself the opportunity to quiet your mind and connecting on a more divine ground. This allows your mind to make new conceptions of your location in the universe. This opportunity provides an understanding of all of your struggles as a whole. When we pray at **Step A**, we can use this opportunity to center ourselves accepting who we are in this process allowing the chance to become more aware. This will certainly help with stress. We then get to express thanks for the blessings that have come our way.

Breathe in and say thank you for being able to breath air no matter how fresh or polluted it is. Breathe out and say a prayer for forgiveness for the things that have taken place on this trip through life. It is important to forgive in order for full healing to occur. Prayer helps to make connections to the rest of the world and to other people as I pray for my wife, daughter, mother, brother, and father. This prayer has the ability to bring me closer to my family. I personally created a packet of prayers which I recite each morning. This prayer packet assists with the habit of consistency and completion as its visibility forces my constant performance when I happen to see it.

Not Religious - No Problem

However, if you are not religious or do not believe in the existence of a higher power, it is totally fine to take this time to disregard ALL of your personal concerns. **This strategy of thinking actually goes for everyone.** This is your first opportunity to clear your mind, and it must take place first thing in the morning. Clear your mind of everything and do not touch your phone or any other device that connects you to the world. Do not think about problems with bills, a research paper that is due, a problem with your partner, or problems in the real world like a tornado in Kansas or an avalanche in Alaska. In order to ensure that this hindrance of thinking does not happen, make sure that you do not touch your phone or computer during this process as it is extremely important to entirely detach from your world. This detachment is mandatory even if your past morning ritual involved being updated in the world of social media. Wait until time permits.

B. AFFIRM – THE AFFIRMATION HABIT

The second letter **A for Affirm** or **Step B** is essential to the preparation process. Affirmations are simple and necessary as they are used to combat negative thinking. Subconsciously all-day long, we program our minds with the things, negative or positive, that we are thinking. For example, imagine you are walking in the door at home and you trip through the doorway. In your mind, you immediately think, "I am so clumsy," or you ask yourself, "How could you do that?" These negative thoughts are extremely damaging to the psyche. These thoughts are negative and do not reflect reality. Reality is simple and much different from this thinking. Reality is that you tripped through the doorway. This action, even if performed every day, does not prove that you are clumsy in any way. This just proves that you trip every day. Is this habit avoidable? Very possibly, but have you attempted to fix the problem before taking on the title of clumsy?

Affirmations combat this irrational thinking by replacing negative irrational thoughts with positive reaffirming thoughts. Nevertheless, affirmations are only effective once they become habit. The affirmation process should be timed. Beginners should start with three to five minutes on the clock, advanced should begin with six to eight minutes, and experts should go ahead with nine to ten minutes.

There are some that do not believe in affirmations. They do not have any belief in their value, but I personally use them and bathe in their benefits. Affirmation critics believe them to be impractical, over-optimistic thinking, but if you look at the process with an open mind, it is easy to see the power in this repetitive programming exercise. Scientifically proven, there is much value in affirmations. I have taught many students that strongly believe in the negative things that they tell themselves every day. They consistently tell themselves, "I am so stupid," "I just can't do it," "I'm too shy to do well," "I'm not good at anything," or "I am so ugly," which in all cases, these thoughts are **ALWAYS** untrue. They are never true in all cases and easy to be seen if **Relentless Positive Perception** is applied. Psychiatrist, best-selling author, and motivational speaker, Dr. Walter E. Jacobson, provides his stance on the value of affirmations as he states, "What we believe on a subconscious level can have a significant impact on the outcome of events." Helping to control what you subconsciously believe about yourself, or at least attempting to, will have significant impact on both your conscious and unconscious thinking.

So how do you go about the process of performing affirmations?

Affirmations are simple. Once again, I personally create a list of multiple affirmations and place them in a packet (after prayers), which assists in the habitual process. Your list of affirmations can be unique to your exact weaknesses or general in context. The reading of these affirmations must be spoken aloud at least three times a day, timed each time beginning with at least five minutes. Set up your environment the same as if you are meditating and begin by breathing in deeply to clear the mind. Take at least five deep breaths, inhaling and exhaling to a count of ten. Read and speak your affirmations from the heart, focusing on each and every word. Believe that your words are true even if they may not be true at the time. They will become true, and you must know this. I use several types of affirmations, like money, self-love, success, and inner peace. They all serve different purposes.

These affirmations can revise and reprogram your thinking patterns, inspiring you to act and think differently. Affirmations will raise confidence, control negative feelings, improve self-esteem, improve productivity, and assist in overcoming bad habits. Affirmations are effective when they are distinct to you and particular to what you desire to achieve, change, or overcome during your mountain process. General, non-specific affirmations are also effective, being that anything will help combat negative thoughts.

Negative thoughts can kill dreams, so they have the ability to kill mentally. They also are responsible for death, so they also possess the ability to kill physically. In order to effectively use affirmations, you will need to evaluate the situations or behaviors that you would like to change about your life. Your affirmations should address all aspects of your life. A general list will assist with this step in the process. Remember that this process is timed and also remember to repeat your affirmations several times throughout your day, especially when you feel yourself falling into negativity.

C. MEDITATE – GYMNASTICS FOR THE BRAIN

The third letter **M for Meditate** or **Step C** is vital to improving and changing your life. This is not the clichéd statement that meditation is everything. However, I must say that it is. If done right, meditation has massive benefits and can lead to happy living. Meditation is another activity that must be done in a consistent fashion to reap the full benefits of the art craft. You cannot meditate some days and experience the advantages. Meditation, if done right, has vast benefits—some being stress reduction, anxiety control, positive emotional health, enhanced self-awareness, increased focus, improved sleep, pain management, and self-control. There are many more benefits to meditation. True meditation is rather difficult, but as stated earlier, practice makes perfect or at least it causes a habitual event to take place. First, it is important to find a quiet place when you are just beginning. This is why it is extremely vital to complete this process during your very *early* morning when most of time, you can find absolute peace and quiet.

The most important tip when meditating is to focus on breathing at all times. Focusing on breathing will force your mind to lock in on only what it should, which is absolutely nothing. When you make meditation a habit, you can perform this exercise anywhere. Meditation has so many benefits that it is compared to mental gymnastics or mental weightlifting. Finding and watching instructional YouTube videos will assist in mastering the process of meditation. When you first begin, you are more than likely to face hardships as it is difficult to lock your focus in on absolutely nothing.

It is inevitable that you will run into roadblocks, but as you continue this process, you will slowly see success. Indian yogi, mystic, and author, Sadhguru Jaggi Vasudev, or simply Sadhguru, once stated, "If we can make just 1% of the population meditative, this world will be a different place." He says this because meditation has the power to change your world and the world that surrounds you. It is important to have positive habits instead of a life full of negative thoughts, negative experiences, and negative practices. Get into the mental gym and meditate despite what you believe about it. The results will blow you away!

D. EVALUATE – LEAVING NEGATIVITY IN THE REARVIEW MIRROR

For some people, this step is one of the hardest because it involves making decisions that can affect you emotionally. This step sometimes involves evaluating family members, but understand it is a mandatory exercise that must be performed. Evaluation of life's negativity is crucial as sometimes we may unconsciously and consciously allow negativity to comfortably reside in our lives. This negativity may come in the form of people or come from people who can be friends, associates, and/or family members. In order to be successful during your mountainous adventures, like branches and vines, you must learn to cut out the people that pull you down. Sometimes we have a tendency to keep people in our lives because we know them, have known them a long time, or feel that we owe them something, but in order to stay focused on progression, we must cut out the things that distract us or restrict our ascension toward success.

Instinctive Response to Drowning

A perfect comparison to this situation is when a person is close to drowning, their body enters a condition that attempts to prevent the drowning from taking place. This bodily condition is an unconscious reaction called *instinctive drowning response*. This condition forces the body to automatically go into a mode where the arms on the body flap and paddle, causing the head to drive itself back. This condition causes extreme danger to the rescuer as there have been many cases of rescuers drowning while attempting to save someone who is drowning. Despite the rescuers' good intentions, they are sometimes killed by their intent. This situation is similar when dealing with toxic people. Toxic or negative people can force you to drown even if your intentions to help or save them came from a good place. These people can pull you down, being that their purpose in life is to cause turmoil and drown those around them.

Deleting Destructive People

Initially when in the learning stage, it is very difficult to avoid or cut out destructive people, but this is an action that must be done. This cutting out can mean avoiding them until they catch the hint, certifiably and officially ending the relationship, or initiating absolute darkness, which means deleting their existence from your life and going dark. Each of the options will have their repercussions and consequences as some could be extreme, but as initially stated, this separation must be done in order to leave the negativity behind. Author and poet, John Mark Green, expresses his thoughts on toxic people as he says, "Toxic people adhere as concrete blocks to your ankles, then push you to swim in poisoned waters." Destructive and negative people do not have good intentions for your success even though it may appear like they do.

These toxic and destructive people are good at making others feel sorry for them, causing a shift in control and allowing openings for manipulation. Even great leader, Mahatma Gandhi, highly regarded the idea of denying access as he once stated, "I will not allow anyone to walk in my mind with dirty feet." This statement is poetic but straightforward, based on the fact that we are aware that we cannot control the actions of others, but we can control the impact of these individuals' actions on ourselves. No one should be allowed to walk around in your life with dirty feet. So it is essential to consistently evaluate your surroundings and more specifically, those who surround you.

The evaluation stage is principal because you must always consistently increase the standards that you set for yourself and restrict direct access to your inner circle. We must make the tough decisions that continue to move us forward. Sometimes we pay too much attention to the destruction instead of the destroyer, which in all cases, is the cause of the destruction. This misguided approach is incorrect. Remember to expect the consequences of any and every action and remember that words are verbal thoughts that reflect the speaker. Always keep in mind that *you* control the impact of the words that are said to *you*. You cannot ever control the actions of others because others will always do what they want to do, but you can have complete control over how to *feel* about what they have done. The great Dalai Lama said it best about the negative ones in your world as he declared, "Let go of negative people. They only show up to share complaints, problems, disastrous stories, fear, and judgment on others. If somebody is looking for a bin to throw all their trash into, make sure it's not your mind." Make sure that you are not being someone else's trash dump and that the people present in your life add positive value and not negativity.

Make sure to always take a step back to evaluate your conversations with friends, verifying if the conversations are worthwhile. This is one of the easiest places to notice everyone's level of life commitment and care for you. If your thoughts and feelings are often disregarded or you are often left feeling emotionally assaulted, decisions must be made. We often allow people to steal our emotional energy, replacing it with their emotional trash. It is critical to make sure that the people that you keep around possess similar goals and have positive traits that you can benefit from. Know that you will also be providing essential traits as this should be the basis for most associations while on the excursion of life. When I was younger, I was told by my favorite teacher to pick my friends like I pick my fruit. This quote would help guide my interactions through the rest of my relationships based on the fact that I have been always extremely happy and successful with my produce choices.

E. REFLECT – MAKING YOU BETTER TOMORROW

The **(R)** reflection step or Step E is not a repeat of **Chapter 4**. This step is only concerned with yesterday. You are to only focus on the previous day. This step makes a person ready to take on their day. How *will* you be better today? How *can* you be better today? What goals will you annihilate today? What are you thankful for this morning? What specifically do you want to accomplish today? What stood out from yesterday? What surprised you yesterday and why? What did you learn from yesterday? Why was it important, and why do you think so? When were you at your best yesterday? What failures can you admit? Did you use your time wisely, and were there moments when you were not effective? How did you work on your goal yesterday and for how long? The answers to these questions will start you on the correct path to an incredible reflection process. Do not skip any of the questions and answer them with sincerity.

This step can and should be completed in a journal. The process of finding and buying a journal is an exhilarating experience. It is important to find something that speaks to your personality. The journal is your canvas. Your personal reflections are the painting of your thoughts on paper. It is essential to be as honest as possible when answering the questions and when you are reflecting in general. There is great value in this early morning reflection. Iyanla Vanzant details the importance of examining the self as she professes, "The journey into self-love and self-acceptance must begin with self-examination… until you take the journey of self-reflection, it is almost impossible to grow or learn in life." True growth only happens after reflection, so take your time to prepare to grow. Journaling can and will have a powerful impact on your existence, and the benefits are immediate, of course, after a habitual routine is established.

Once again, developing this skill is not optional as journaling will prepare your mind for the journeys to come. Journaling has many benefits, such as increasing creativity, optimizing positivity, accelerating the ability to manifest goals, helping to recover from the mountain processes of the past, purging the mind, increasing focus, and so many more. This is why you must not skip the **R** or the reflection process. Once the process has become a part of your morning ritual, it will become easier for the words to flow from your mind to paper like water over dirty dishes.

F. MOTIVATE – METAPHYSICAL FOOD FOR THE SPIRIT

The second **letter M,** the final but favorite letter of the morning ritual, is designed to provide the mind with motivational food for thought and the body with emotional fuel to move once actual stored energy has run out. This is the last leg of the morning routine because it pushes you out the door with purpose and forces you to move with an attitude ready and equipped to defeat all the obstacles of your upcoming day. Motivation is as necessary as breakfast, but like breakfast, most people skip it because the benefits are not truly realized. If the importance of breakfast was fully realized, everyone would eat it despite what is going on in their everyday lives. The same understanding must be applied when supplying the mind, body, and soul with daily motivation. I have seen, experienced, and applied the tenants of motivational videos and/or inspirational readings to my daily life and have received major benefits and mental advantages due to this decision.

Motivation is extremely important but difficult to consistently keep going every day. The number one reason that we fail at reaching our goals is due to lack of motivation, purpose, and drive. Motivation is one of the keys to success, and without it, it is impossible to be successful. Based on this understanding, the management of your motivation is a critical element to your success. High motivation leads to a higher output of energy. Increased motivation can lead to overcoming the impossible, being that motivation can push a person through their ceilings. When an individual is motivated, the only thing that can block their path is death. Understand that this step allows for more control over your existence. *Being able to motivate yourself is a fundamental skill as your personal productivity depends on it.* Think about all of the steps connecting and working together to satisfy a common goal. There are many great speakers that you can listen to on YouTube from Eric Thomas, Inky Johnson, Les Brown, Tony Robbins, Robert Kiyosaki, Grant Cardone, Susan Powter, David Goggins, and Mel Robbins. I even have a few videos available.

The influence of an individual's needs and desires both impact the direction of their future behavior. It is important to guide and be in control of your own motivation. Do not depend on others to motivate you. As I stated before, *you* must care for *you*. You must first value yourself more than anyone else before you can value others. How can you show others true love when you cannot understand how to unconditionally love yourself? You must move you by knowing how to inspire yourself. The motivational videos will provide daily inspiration and positive information.

The **PAMERM Process** is similar to a ladder because without the step before, the next step becomes harder and depending on the height, reaching it is impossible. Once this morning routine becomes habit, you will then be ready for your day and any mountains that come your way.

III. STASH YOUR BAGS EVEN IF YOU DO NOT HAVE ANYTHING

The importance of having a stash somewhere cannot be overemphasized. Develop the habit of keeping a little money aside when the going seems good. This will invariably help you in tough times. We cannot predict the future, but we can prepare for it. Nothing can make an already difficult situation more difficult than money problems. Make it a point to always ensure that your finances are in order at all times to avoid complicating an already difficult situation. Always have a budget and constantly attempt to clear up unpaid bills when you are in the mountain-free period. It is even wise if you pay bills like rent and some yearly subscriptions ahead of time. This will come in handy.

Put money away and don't touch it for anyone or anything!

Put together a spreadsheet to balance and save your money like a business does. You have to consider yourself a working company. American businessman and radio host, Dave Ramsey, wisely states, "You must gain control over your money or the lack of it will forever control you." Like I stated earlier, it is important to control the things that you can control, which at most points is everything in your life. You must always be accountable for all your activities, especially your finances. The biggest question is how do you save money if you do not have any? There are multiple ways to begin saving. I will list my top strategies below:

1. It is *essential to pay yourself first.* Start putting a bit of money away into an account other than your main account. Send miscellaneous unsullied money into this account before any bills or anything else is paid. Make sure not to check on this account's progress and let the money build.
2. Create a side hustle and save this money. It's important to find your creative talent. There must be a way to create an additional stream of income by showcasing one of your many talents. The money earned from your additional talents must go directly in the account mentioned in #1.
3. Do not obsess about saving money as it can be counterproductive, but as I stated initially, make paying yourself first a normal event.
4. Run your finances like a business. Your budget must be produced on a spreadsheet similar to one used by a business. The more detailed you are, the better off you will be.
5. Be in full control of your spending but don't die from hunger. Don't sacrifice necessities.

6. Prioritize spending and evaluate finances. Do not let food expenses equate to over 60 percent of your spending. Realize that your needs down the road should go first, not second, on the list of priorities.
7. Do not overcomplicate your finances. It is simple. You must not spend more than you make.
8. Remember and never forget what being broke feels like. This moment should be used a bookmark, and the feeling should be used as gas.
9. Throw all extra change into your savings account mentioned in #1. This relates to any money that you would normally spend on unnecessary somethings.
10. Minimize credit card expenses as much as possible trying to keep charges lower than an established goal like 40 percent. This must be discussed with paper or your life partner in order to understand ways to pay more and decrease overall monthly payments.
11. Believe that you will be successful in saving. Keeping a positive perspective and mindset about finances will help in not becoming mentally low when things go wrong.

It is important to take responsibility for your life, which includes your finances. Taking control of your finances is exceptionally significant to being ready for your future mountains.

IV.   FIND YOUR PARAGON: WHO IS YOUR PERFECT EXAMPLE?

Who inspires you? When you journal, you will identify what inspires you, but now the question of the hour is what outside source provides your motivation? Keeping examples of your definition of perfection handy are remarkably paramount to your preparation process. When we were children, it was easy to notice the people we admired and idolized. This step does not in any way refer to fanning over people but having mentors available to assist in your production as a person. Virtual or physical mentors, teachers, and/or role models are necessary in helping you become the ultimate you. Your mentor does not have to be someone that you know personally, but it is vital to have one.

The idea of having mentors is timeless as great Greek philosopher, Epictetus, advises, "One of the best ways to elevate your character is to emulate worthy role models." The most important life lessons will come from your paragons because you naturally value this person. Paragons teach us how to live and put the best effort forward. Paragons push us to believe and live beyond the bounds of possibility.

If the paragon is physical, make sure it's a person that you can trust whether it is with secrets or personal problems. This person might not necessarily be a blood relative, but the kind of bond and mutual care shared with people like them makes them family. Always make sure that this connection is strong. You never know what might happen when things get rough. We do need people in life as human interaction is necessary to our existence. During your good days, ensure that you are a source of help to others. If you do this, you can be rest assured that you will have people to lean on in your own times of need, especially if you have already rid your circle of the negative influences.

If the mentor is virtual, make sure to seek their motivation as often as possible throughout your day because their words are available anytime you need them. This virtual role model provides a standard to compare ourselves with. Some of the role models can be the same individuals that you watch during your motivational morning routine or authors from your favorite inspirational books, but it is required to have positive role models in place. Nearly every successful individual has publicly revealed that they have had positive role models that they've based their lives. These people lead their lives attempting to duplicate the successes of these individuals. Author, Charles Dickens, said it best, "No one is useless in this world who lightens the burdens of another." These individuals have been placed on earth as guides, so do not hesitate to utilize their services. It is your personal responsibility to discover and assemble a team of paragons to emulate, and it is overly important to carefully choose the members of your team.

V.   PRACTICE RELENTLESS POSITIVE PERCEPTION (R.P.P.)

Positive thinking and success goes hand in hand. Depression and stress are caused by outside influences or negative thoughts produced by the brain. Based on the known details about stress and depression, negative thinking doesn't just affect the mind, but it also impacts the body, sometimes even causing death. Based on this idea, it is hugely of interest to stay protected from negativity and negative thinking. Positive perception possesses the ability to eliminate all forms of damaging thoughts from the brain. **Relentless Positive Perception** does not in any way mean to live in an unworldly bliss but more plainly means to approach bad situations from a positive standpoint. The cup is always half-full because you will undoubtedly keep it full, and this is something that you must know and never forget. Doubt is a clear sign and an indication that you do not fully believe, so you must attempt to do your best to avoid this emotion. Extreme optimism is the cure to the disease of doubt.

There are several ways to consistently work on your **RPP**, and they are as follows:

1. Laugh and smile as often as possible by opening yourself to humor and keeping yourself open to humor.
2. Keep your thoughts off negativity or harping over bad things that take place during your day. Revert back to one. Remember you are in control of your thoughts.
3. Find positive videos to watch or find inspirational books to read at several points during your day.
4. Find two- to three-minute moments throughout your day to meditate.
5. Plot out check-in moments throughout your day to evaluate how you are feeling.
6. Keep positive people in your circle and avoid negative influences and/or people. This must be evaluated constantly throughout your day. Pay attention to your feelings when around certain people.
7. Be aware of the things that cause you to revert back to negative states and be aware of your emotional state throughout your day. If you truly focus on it, you will notice it.
8. Stay consistent and make this a habit.

RPP has many health benefits, like increased life span, decreased rates of depression and stress, greater opposition to common illnesses, better cardiovascular benefits, like reduced death from heart-related illnesses, and better handling of hardships (mountains) once encountered. It is important to consistently practice ***RPP*** throughout your day, and the benefits will automatically impact your life.

VI. CONTEMPLATE HYPOTHETICALS

In preparation for the next mountain or mountains, it is important to think about the future situations that can and will occur. You have to be careful not to begin "catastrophizing" in which you imagine a complete catastrophe out of situations that will occur or may never occur at all. Instead, you must prepare your mind and body to train for your approaching trauma. This training for trauma is vital and virtually practiced everywhere in the business world, but unfortunately, it is not practiced enough in our everyday lives.

In education, based on the increased occurrences of school shootings in the United States, staff and students are now training with their local police departments and learning how to quickly handle these emergency situations. Because of this, the victim count and violent incidences have drastically decreased even though they still take place. Flight attendants, doctors, police officers, fire people, and nurses all receive some kind of disaster training, which has proven benefits, like reducing danger, distress, panic, and casualties. This is the main reason for fire, evacuation, and/or any local emergency drills. Imagine a situation where this practice has never taken place and an actual fire or the unpracticed emergency arises. Based on the idea that no one is familiar with procedure, the incident could be disastrous.

The same understanding can be applied to your life, especially if you treat every problem as a surprise. One of the greatest presidents of the United States, Abraham Lincoln, was once famously quoted, "Give me six hours to chop down a tree and I will spend the first four sharpening the axe." Lincoln knew the importance of planning and preparing. A properly sharpened ax can quickly chop down a tree, and a dull ax is pretty much useless. So sharpen the ax, and the tree is down in a few chops. This is the idea of working smarter, not harder. In engineering, the design process is to ask, imagine, plan, create, and improve. Our steps are similar due to the fact that nearly identical procedures can also be applied to your life.

You have a responsibility to be prepared to act on your trauma when it arrives. You can start by beginning to ask the necessary questions almost as if you are performing a professional assessment. Some of the questions can be, what emergency plan can you put into effect if things go wrong? What is your recovery plan if a catastrophe were to take place? Are there any plans currently in place for my upcoming traumas? After the questions are asked and answered, the planning begins. Once the plan is created, it must be periodically reviewed in order to improve on the plans. There is never a perfect plan of action, but having a plan is always better than not having one and being surprised. After this is done, you can move on to creating the necessary solutions. Always jump on the opportunity to sharpen your ax and make sure to take your time doing so.

VII. POSITIVE SELF-TALK

"You will become what you think about most; your success or failure in anything, large or small, will depend on your programming – what you accept from others, and what you say when you talk to yourself." Shad Helmstetter stated this in his book, *"What to Say When You Talk to Yourself."* The skill of positive self-talk when paired with **Relentless Positive Perception** can make your palace of positivity indestructible. Just like affirmations, we talk to ourselves all day long, especially during our waking hours. It is essential to communicate with yourself as positive as you can to repel and resist negative emotions while building your self-confidence. Just because a person is unaware of the influence of bad and destructive conversation does not mean that it does not severely affect them. This negative self-talk can unconsciously reflect and emulate exactly what the person regularly receives from others or from themselves on a daily basis. If a parent repeatedly calls their child dumb or stupid, the child will most likely call themselves and/or refer to themselves by the same negative names or have a hard time seeing past the names that they are often called. As a result, this victim will identify as these names and act as such. As an educator, I often interact with these damaged individuals on a daily basis, attempting to erase lifetimes of painful speech and hurtful embedded thoughts. Dealing with this embedded pain has now become one of the hardest parts of my job.

When we have so many negative interactions, we begin to transform from these traumatic situations, developing patterns of negative thinking, which leads to programmed negative self-talk. Many believe that talking to oneself is a sign of a mental disorder, but many others and I strongly disagree. Positive self-talk is designed to defeat the negative name-calling that we often subconsciously do on a daily basis. Positive self-talk is huge at helping to prepare for the mountains of life because it impacts our entire surroundings and the way we view the world. Positive self-talk dramatically changes our perspective, helping to improve our self-confidence, self-image, and self-esteem. The affirmations that I perform each morning are considered forms of self-talk and are extremely valuable to jump-starting my day. The self-talk that I complete during the day provides motivation and other side benefits. Getting rid of the mind critic is one of the most productive ways to prepare for anything, and in doing so, you will become an indestructible fortress of positivity.

VIII.   READING TO ARM THE BRAIN

They say do not bring a knife to a gunfight and imagine if this scenario really happened. Oh, no! This scene definitely doesn't end well for the knife holder unless the person is a Mighty Morphin Power Ranger (No pun intended.). So, in life in order to be ready, it is important to have the proper tools necessary to defend yourself. As a former reading specialist, the importance of reading cannot be described in words. However, it is scary to see the overall drastic decline of this activity. In the U.S., leisure reading or reading for fun is at an all-time low. The availability of social media, television, and video games distracts and takes up a lot of the time an individual could be utilizing to read.

As a teacher, we have experienced extremely low amounts of educational reading as at-home participation is devastatingly decreasing each year. The statistics behind these observations are very scary, especially when thinking about the future of society. Reading is necessary in developing one's comprehension and critical thinking, but most importantly, one's imagination. When watching television or videos, you are depending on another person's given images, thereby allowing your imagination to be programmed. Social media and television are not the signs of Armageddon, but we must limit ourselves by giving ourselves the fuel needed to become our own versions of greatness. We are born with our own version of creativity, and reading enhances this ability inside each of us. So, in order to arm yourself in preparation for the upcoming mountains of life, you must read, arming your brain for the fight that is sure to come looking for you.

Reading is exercise for the mind, and there are plenty of available books that can help you to get ready for the issues in life. There are books available for every interest you possess. If television interests you, there is a book based on your favorite genre of movies. Go and fall in love with a book and spend time with an author. This is self-education at its finest. Even if you read thirty minutes a day, you will see massive benefits, like the ability to live a happier life, defeat depression, increase your levels of empathy and tolerance, create a broader perspective, and fight mental decline as you age, just to name a few.

Reading is a must, and this activity cannot be skipped for any reason. The belief that there is not enough time available is not at all acceptable. Plan out your reading and stuff it into your schedule by any means necessary. The problems, troubles, struggles, successes, and/or questions in life are somewhere written in some book. Information is gold, so start digging. This world is not new, and the mountains of now have been here since the beginning of time despite new innovations like technology. Read to arm yourself against it all.

IX. ALWAYS HAVE A BACKUP PLAN

Finally, not be cliché, but you should make sure that you always have a plan B for any situation in life. I know many are being instructed to not have a backup plan, but having a backup plan is like giving yourself a lifeline. We all must have played a video game at one point in our life, and having additional lifelines while playing help us to understand how valuable lifelines can be, especially when we make it to a stage that was so difficult to reach. A lifeline will always come in handy to ensure that we successfully finish the stage and cross over to the next one. There have been many times when I'm playing a difficult stage in a video game and I must lose in order to win. I am afforded the opportunity to make a mistake. This error or loss produced a chance for me to understand and become familiarized with the obstacle. If there is only one life or credit available when playing a difficult stage, then every step must be carefully calculated. This same idea applies to your life situations. Ensure you have a plan B or a pivot point that will aid in the successful completion of your life journey. Are you traveling in your car? Keep some money for extra fuel or bus trip in case your car breaks down or you have to take a different route. Are you working on an important project on your laptop? Continuously save a copy of your work on the cloud or a flash drive in case your laptop acts up as we all have experienced the frustration of losing everything. Use this way of thinking when you are creating scenarios in order to have solutions available beforehand. This backup strategy will definitely ensure your successful completion of any task at hand.

Mountain! Where Are You? Oh, there you are!

My childhood friend, Ben, does not ever want to go back into state custody, so he has been preparing every day while living his life making sure to avoid any familiar circumstances that endangers his success. He remembers the pain of the past and never wants his children to have to experience the same kinds of circumstances. Ben is now happily married with two boys. He is a walking example of manhood for his children. He is the perfect example of a husband for his wife. Ben often reflects back on his past, but he does not regret his experiences. He uses his experiences as the answers that inspire his existence and orders the direction he gives to his two boys.

Ben prepares solutions to problems ahead of experiencing them. He works hard to provide for his family. He cooks dinner for his wife at least three times a week to give her a break. Ben wants to show his wife that he cares about her day and her overall sanity. He always thinks about how to work things out so that he doesn't overwhelm his wife, who has chaotic days, being that she works in healthcare. He sometimes gets his boys to help him cook, and they all wash the dishes as a family on the days he prepares dinner. Ben also spends time with his boys by calculating and planning out this time on a weekly basis. He uses all of the experiences to bond with his boys because he did not have a father. He has a system set up that prevents or attempts to prevent future problems. This process is not a sure fix, but at least it is an attempt to prevent future obstacles. This type of flexibility is vital to life.

On the other hand, Sam has been surviving college only because she realized that she has experienced worse situations.

The chaos of the college experience is lightweight compared to what she has endured and encountered earlier in life. College is a small mountain compared to what she is used to. She has recycled her pain, transformed it into passion, and now uses it to propel herself to success. She has continuously been on the dean's list since she has been at the university and has been working hard to study for the MCAT. She has destined herself for greatness.

Think about if you applied the tenets of the mountain process and compared your largest mountain accomplishments to whatever you are currently experiencing. They normally will not compare because you have already experienced success, so use your energy to expect the mountains of tomorrow. Expectations of the mountains of tomorrow are essential to overcoming them. It is paramount to prepare for today, yesterday, and it is equally essential to prepare for tomorrow, today. The best and the only way to control your future is to prepare for it now.

Chapter Eight

ANOTHER MOUNTAIN AWAITS

"After climbing a great hill, one only finds that there are many more hills to climb."
– **Nelson Mandela**

Now that you have successfully completed your mountain task and have overcome your obstacle, it is time to look ahead and move forward. It is time to pick yourself back up and continue life's journey. You have done a good job of getting your past problem out of the way. So by all means, move ahead with pride and confidence. As you take a breath of relief and walk with happy steps, you look forward, and what do you see? Another mountain!

We are not promised easy lives. However, we are guaranteed to run into problems, obstacles, and mishaps. If we follow the proper steps, we are guaranteed to crush the things that get in our way.

As you headed down your last mountain and finally reached the other side, you were so focused on the last steps of your journey that you did not realize that another massive mountain was waiting for you. Funnily enough, there will also be another mountain waiting after you climb down the next one and another one after that. This sequence of problems may make you want to give up and force you to choose the earlier options of one, two, or three as you figure that there's no way to consider choosing option four and climb another mountain. Life does not change, pause, or give you a chance to catch your breath just because you finished handling a huge problem. Some people might have the luxury of not running into another mountain for several thousand life miles or kilometers. However, others will run directly into a new mountain right after their feet touch the new ground. This is the vicious cycle of life, but you must walk against the current to become stronger. So walk along!

When thinking back to Oprah Winfrey's story, it's easy to see that her problems, too, came in succession. The same sequences happened to my friend, Ben, and my former student, Sam. Early on, they all experienced monstrous mountain after monstrous mountain. Think about your life and the problems you have encountered. Have your problems struck in vicious patterns, or have they occurred one at a time?

Think about it like this. After conquering your last mountain, you are now considered the champion, and champions must defend their titles anytime they are challenged. This is why every year there are NBA Playoffs, Champions League Finals, Europa League Finals, The US Open, Formula One, NFL Super Bowl, MLB World Series, UFC Championships, WWE World Heavyweight Champion, and so many other regular title defense events. Title defenses are ongoing, and participants must prove themselves on a regular basis to retain their spot at the top. This is also how it is in the journey of life. Once you finally overcome one obstacle, another awaits. The next mountain is there to challenge what you've learned and to provide more knowledge and power. It wants your title. Your journey does not stop at winning one title unless you plan to be a one-hit wonder like Bo Bice or the Cleveland Cavaliers (just kidding). In this game called life, in order to remain an active participant, you must also continuously defend your title and prove your credibility by defeating the mountains that you are certain to keep meeting while on life's expedition. In life, it is inevitable that you will continue to meet mountain after mountain. So, what kind of champion will you be? Will you defend your title, or will you run scared?

PRACTICE TO MASTER. PRACTICE TO DECREASE WEAKNESS. PRACTICE TO IMPROVE!

The good news is that, just as they say, practice makes perfect or practice makes permanent, we can apply this idea to the mountains and problems in life. Your plan of action is simple. Since you continue to meet the mountains in your life, master them. Since you continue to run into mountains, run over them. The more you are prepared to overcome your problems, the better you become at tackling the problems that continue to pop up. It is important to work on becoming better each second of your day.

One of the NBA's greatest three-point shooters of all-time, Stephen Curry, possesses an incredible work ethic, and this is no secret. On April 15, 2015, during team basketball practice or afterwards as he normally sticks around hours later than other players working on becoming better, Curry successfully hit a whopping total of seventy-seven three-pointers in a row, finishing the day hitting 94 out of 100 three-point shots. Now fast forward to a few days later and the

Golden State Warriors, Curry's team, are down by 20 points in a playoff game going into the final quarter. Curry does the improbable and wills the team back, hitting three-pointer after three-pointer. Now the game is tied with 9.6 seconds left. The basketball is inbounded and passed to Curry, and he terribly misses the three-point shot. The ball is recovered by his own teammate and with five seconds left, Curry catches the ball and shoots again, and the ball goes directly through the hoop without touching anything but the net. The Warriors win! Upon looking at the replay, it is discovered that during the shot, Curry's eyes were closed. During the practice before this game, Curry hit a total of ninety-four three-pointers, missing only six shots. Because of his hard work in practice, his eyes were no longer needed for this remarkable last shot.

    Curry was only able to bring his team back because of the practice that he put in days prior. Curry was ready for the impossible because he has already gone past everyone else's possible, and this only happened due to consistent practice. He used practice to master the Three-point shot and become a better him. Practice makes perfect, or at least practice trains you to be prepared for anything that comes. Curry's story proves the more you are prepared, the more you are ready for anything, especially the impossible.

HERE WE ARE AGAIN! CLIMB, CLIMB, AND CLIMB!

The experiences and lessons that are automatically absorbed when overcoming your problems in life are there to make you stronger and prepare you for the tasks ahead. Fret not, for you are on the right path and just as you have followed the mountain process to help in defeating your immediate past problem, you will also be victorious when climbing the next one. You will also overcome the one that follows after that one. Life goes on, and the problems come with it. So what.

You never know how your mountain range of problems has been designed but make sure that you journey through it. Remember to climb, climb, and climb! You have all that you need to rise up and conquer all of your mountains, and no problem is too big once you follow the mountain process correctly. However, if you give up climbing through your mountain range of problems too early, you may never realize what Benjamin, Samantha, Angelou, Oprah, Jordan, Jobs, Gates, and many others found out. They realized that success was waiting at the end of the process.

While attending Chicago State University, I had several classes with a woman named Mariel, who eventually became someone I would consider a friend. While we were in college, I watched Mariel experience hardship after hardship during which her grandmother died, her husband cheated on her, she got very sick, and then she lost her job. These events happened in quick succession. Mariel kept asking, "Why me?" She let these events break her down. This entire experience was definitely a hard one, but my only advice for her was to keep moving and don't stop. Unfortunately, Mariel stopped. I would say, "Mariel, keep climbing! That's all that you can do." Mariel stopped climbing. Mariel never recovered from this episode of events and is currently homeless. She never realized that we are all in the same place, suffering and coming from some kind of hardship or at least about to experience one, yet we are all in the same place enduring. She never understood that if we based our future success on the range of obstacles that have already come our way, it would be logically impossible for anyone to become successful. The quote made popular by the great Japanese writer, Haruki Murakami, defines how a human should handle life's experiences as he writes, "Pain is inevitable; suffering is optional." To suffer is a choice and is something that does not have to take place but certainly can and will, especially if an individual dwells in pain. It is important to let pain go and climb the next mountains because you can handle your problems despite how the odds may appear. Mariel wasn't expecting to face all of her issues (mountains) at once.

She wasn't prepared to face any of her issues at all. This lack of expectation and preparation is what eventually led to her downfall and her current homelessness. After enduring a mountain, an obstacle, or a problem, it's important to learn from the experience. Reflection is key, so make sure to reflect on your experiences.

YOU ARE THE IMPOSSIBLE! WHY NOT YOU?

Never ask the question, "Why me?" Rather, you must say, "Why not me?" Remember that mountains are the solutions to your weaknesses. Mountains force you to become stronger. In the next chapter, we will discuss the importance of using your past to fuel your future. Expect your problems as these problems are meant to be lived, not just solved. You are expected to exist through your problems, so do not get too down on yourself. You can either be Ben, Jordan, Oprah, Curry, or . . . Mariel. We all have the ability to do the impossible and close our eyes when we shoot.

For instance, in a 2009 article by Tara Parker-Pope published in *The New York Times* titled, "The Human Body Is Built For Distance," it was revealed that a human can outrun almost any animal. Okay, not if you are running for your life, and a cheetah is chasing you as that surely will not end well unless you are the world's fastest man, Usain Bolt. However, in a long range 26-mile marathon or 100-mile Iron Man race, people can outdistance almost every animal. Of course, most animals can sprint faster than humans, but people can outrun nearly any animal in existence. This goes to show how resilient humans were built to be. You were built to cancel out the word, impossible. Human beings are, therefore, one of the strongest and smartest mammals in the world. This is not mere speculation but a scientifically proven fact.

You already have the innate ability to achieve the impossible, so why not capitalize on it and improve yourself? Outspoken author, Marianne Williamson, rightly said, "The top of one mountain is always the bottom of another." Another mountain awaits… so what! Let's climb it! There are a multitude of mountains lined up in your way? So what! Let's climb them! You just came down from a grueling task of overcoming your present mountain? So what! You feel tired and hurt? So what! You get my point?

You need to push on and get over the next mountain because that is how life is designed to be. Life is a journey of mountains, and it's important to always be ready to climb them. Use the strategies presented in this book and apply them to your life, and you can overcome any mountain that comes your way.

Chapter Nine

THE NEXT LEVEL; USING YOUR PAST TO BECOME A GREATER YOU

> "Sometimes people make it seem like you have to have certain prerequisites or a crazy life story in order to be successful in this world. But the truth is you really don't."
> –**Stephen Curry**

Many times we tend to devalue the lessons we learn from our obstacles, and we also fail to understand how a seemingly insignificant bump in the road can play a major role in elevating and assisting us to reach the next level. We assume the people who have achieved greatness have some special stars attached to them or have somehow fell into a unique journey that was purposely meant for them and their guaranteed success. Although this might be true, because there is supposed to be some uniqueness in every person's life journey and mountains that come with it, the fact still remains that each person's mountain is there as a stepping stone to help them reach the next level.

What this means is that everyone has some sort of unique journey on their way to success, but in the end, all the different paths lead to the same goal, which is becoming the best version of yourself. So, no mountain is insignificant. All mountains matter! Every single mountain whether a hill or Everest itself is vital to your success. You should strive to fully grasp the lesson that each mountain experience is there to teach so that you can use it as a springboard to attaining your next level.

Many of my students are obsessed with the National Basketball Association or as the world knows it, the NBA. They love talking about their favorite players, and having discussions about which player is better. Conversations usually turn into heated debates as they discuss which team is the greatest of all-time. They debate that Michael Jordan is better than Kobe Bryant but not better than Lebron James (not true by the way). They discuss the top crossover dribble and slam dunk highlights from the night before. I usually end these conversations almost immediately. Most of the time, these talks are only conversations driven by emotion, not by fact during which I inject verities like Stephen Curry's workout routine, Jordan's no-quit attitude, Kobe's hard work, or Lebron's summer regime. These details are rarely a subject of thought and debate when I hear these basketball conversations.

I am usually irritated and annoyed with these conversations because I notice that people often obsess over the result of excessive hard work but never pay attention to the steps a person takes to become their version of *great*. Their steps toward becoming the world's greatest in their chosen fields oftentimes always involve the completion of the strenuous mountain process. Ask Stephen Curry, Michael Jordan, Oprah Winfrey, Maya Angelou, Albert Einstein, Jim Carrey, Richard Branson, Bill Gates, Steve Jobs, Stephen King, Monique Rodriguez, Jay-Z... and the list goes on. Each one of these individuals has overcome the greatest possible obstacles, but their experience through the *process* and how they applied it in their life's journey is what eventually led to their success. An African proverb says, "No person is born great, great people become great when others are sleeping." Are you the sleeper, or are you the one awake doing all of the work? Are you one of the ones awake working on becoming great?

THE PETER GRIFFIN SYNDROME

The *process* is necessary for creating the ultimate you. Endurance and resilience are gained after each completion (mountain) to ultimately make you your best possible version.

This *process* is one of the keys to life. To become better with each moment. To become better with each second. A better you is necessary, especially if you seek success. This is why enjoying the process is important. Most of the world's most successful people have subconsciously learned to appreciate their mountain processes and discovered that the mountains were there to help them become who they are today. It is your turn to use your mountain to get yourself to the next level and avoid using your problems to entangle you into a depressive state.

Instead of allowing your mountains to discourage you, let your mountains encourage you. Instead of letting your mountains drag you down, let your mountains elevate you. Let these situations expose you to the reality that you are tougher and more resilient than you think you are. Let these events teach you that life without obstacles is equivalent to a life without ever reaching your full potential as to be challenged is prime to becoming better altogether. Go play your favorite game on the easiest difficulty and watch the fun and interest slip out the backdoor. Experiencing challenges is essential to growth. Let your mountains teach you that even through traumatic events or stress, you should respond with the tactics, outlooks, and perspectives provided in this book.

Mariel still looks at pain as a hurdle but does not jump over it, and this is why she is still where she is today. Mariel allowed pain, challenge, and hurt end her progression. She has labeled herself as a victim, and instead of being victorious against the mountain, she has quit the race and given up climbing mountains. However, despite all of her running and resistance, her mountains are still there. She began the race to success and was on route to finishing, but unfortunately, she allowed life to win. Life punched her right in the throat, and she fell down.

Presently, Mariel is still down. She is still holding her knee like she is Peter Griffin from the animated cartoon, *Family Guy*. I have coined this as *The Peter Griffin Syndrome*. *This condition places you in a state of helplessness. After getting knocked down and instead of immediately rising back to your feet, you sit down, cry, and complain.* Getting back up is not even part of the plan, and Mariel has no intention of getting past this point of pain.

She still has not recovered from being down, but the good news is she still has time. She can still follow the mountain process. She can still apply the methods of the mountain, and she can still progress in life. No matter how bad your situation may look, it is never too late to understand that you will become stronger once you climb your mountains. It is never too late to face your mountains but remember your options once you are at the bottom. The only way to fully overcome the mountain you are facing is to use the experience you receive from it to propel yourself to the next level of success.

William Shakespeare once famously said, "Some are born great, some achieve greatness, while others have greatness thrust upon them." It is your time to achieve greatness. Get up, square up to that mountain, and get to climbing. You have all you need to overcome it to become a better you.

CONCLUSION

"It is not the mountain we conquer, but ourselves."
– Sir Edmund Hillary.

It is a common thing to come across obstacles in our quest to achieve the best out of life. Unfortunately, life does not exist without ups and downs. These ups generally are referred to as the good times in life and the downs represent the bad times. But let's look at this idea from another perspective. What if *the only way to get through your downs is to go up and over* the mountains of life? Think about it. When you experience bad situations and are faced with mountains, start climbing.

Don't run away. Don't stare. Don't avoid. Start climbing! And once you get to the top of the mountain, STOP! You must make sure that you look back. Look back at what you have just overcome. Look at what you have just climbed. Many of us suffer from low self-esteem because we have climbed so many mountains in life, but once we get to the top, we hurry up and climb down. But this time, stop. Look back, pat yourself on the back, and appreciate yourself.

Be like the African lizard that fell from the tree unharmed and went on to praise itself when no one else would. Show gratitude – good job, self! Feel good and reflect, but don't forget to keep moving because you are not done yet. You still have to get down the mountain, and many times the last step is the hardest. Many of us are in our last steps of our current circumstances, and now it's hard to finish. This is a normal occurrence, so you must make sure to push hard and finish going over the mountain.

When you finally reach the other side and your feet hit the bottom, you've now graduated from frustration to tiredness. You're breathing hard. You cannot stand, and you cannot catch your breath. You finally feel accomplished. But guess what is waiting for you? Another mountain! This mountain can be bigger, or it can be smaller, but it's a guarantee that another mountain is waiting for you. This is the story of life.

You must understand that when you go through stuff, don't ask the question, "Why me?" You must say, "Why not me?" Because once you ascend the mountain, once you climb your mountain, you will get stronger naturally, and there is nothing you can do about it. The strength you get from successfully climbing your mountain is what will give you the drive to climb future mountains, which are sure to come.

So you must learn to **Expect Mountains** because if you expect them, they won't shock you when you encounter them, and you'll know exactly what to do when you're at the bottom of one. When you eventually overcome your mountain, and the next one, and the one after that, you will find out that you are gradually getting stronger and rising to the next level. After completing this process over and over, you will gradually become a better you. This is the secret of life.

I leave you with the words of Dr. Seuss—"You're off to great places; today is your day. Your mountain is waiting, so get on your way."

ABOUT THE AUTHOR

Shaunwell Posley is President of Posley Global, LLC, Co-founder of Lion's Share Educational Services, and Editor-in-Chief of 95Notes Literary Magazine. He is also an English instructor and head speech coach at Thornton Fractional North High School in Calumet City, IL.

Just nearing his late 30s, Shaunwell has close to thirty years of professional work experience in various sectors as he began working at the age of nine. He has worked in over 10 different fields. In 2006, he co-founded 95Notes Literary Magazine during which he has helped to publish the works of many notable artists and writers worldwide from Japan to Australia to California. He has worked hand-in-hand with some of the most noteworthy poets and writers throughout the world as 95Notes is an internationally recognized publication. In 2009, he developed and designed a customer service department implementing the customer service policy at a Fortune 500 company.

As a teacher, Shaunwell earned the Calumet City Lion's Club Teacher of the Year award for the 2017 - 2018 school year. As a coach, he was awarded sponsor of the Year in 2016 - 2017. As head coach for six years, the speech has broken every school record in existence winning close to 400 medals, 7 team trophies, 5 Conference 2nd place championships, and a 6th place individual event state ranking.

Shaunwell Posley attended Prairie View A&M University for two years. He received his Bachelor's of Arts in English literature from Chicago State University and was awarded a Master's degree in Teaching from National-Louis University.

Shaunwell enjoys reading, writing in serene environments, playing his PS4, traveling with family, and hanging out with his wife and daughter.

ABOUT THE PUBLISHER

Posley Global, LLC is a publishing forum designed to showcase innovative and creative minds throughout the world.

MY PARAGONS

Father - *Robert L. Posley*
Mother - *Lela S. Washington*
NBA Legend - *Kobe Bryant*
Motivational Speaker - *Eric Thomas*
The Great - *Frederick Douglass*

YOUR PARAGONS

I. **Paragon 1**

   1. Who: ....
   2. Why: ....
   3. How can you benefit from your interactions?

      ....

II. Paragon 2

1. Who: ....
2. Why: ....
3. How can you benefit from your interactions?
   ....

III. Paragon 3

1. Who: ....
2. Why: ....
3. How can you benefit from your interactions?
   ....

IV. Paragon 4

1. Who: ....
2. Why: ....
3. How can you benefit from your interactions?
   ....

V. Paragon 5

1. Who: ....
2. Why: ....
3. How can you benefit from your interactions?
   ....

VALUABLE NOTES SECTION

Note taking guide for each chapter:

CHAPTER ONE
The Mountain

1. What is the most important quote from the chapter? What stands out to you the most?

   ....
   ....
   ....

2. Explain why you wrote the quote that you selected.

   ....
   ....
   ....

3. How will apply what you learned to your life? Be exact.

   ....
   ....
   ....

4. Anything else that needs mentioning?

   ....
   ....
   ....

CHAPTER TWO
The Options Before You

1. What is the most important quote from the chapter? What stands out to you the most?

   ....
   ....
   ....

2. Explain why you wrote the quote that you selected.

   ....
   ....
   ....

3. How will apply what you learned to your life? Be exact.

   ....
   ....
   ....

4. Anything else that needs mentioning?

   ....
   ....
   ....

CHAPTER THREE
Climbing the Mountain

1. What is the most important quote from the chapter? What stands out to you the most?

   ....
   ....
   ....
   ....

2. Explain why you wrote the quote that you selected.

   ....
   ....
   ....
   ....

3. How will apply what you learned to your life? Be exact.

   ....
   ....
   ....
   ....

4. Anything else that needs mentioning?

   ....
   ....
   ....
   ....

CHAPTER FOUR
Looking Back: R & C (Reflect & Celebrate)

1. What is the most important quote from the chapter? What stands out to you the most?

   ....
   ....
   ....
   ....

2. Explain why you wrote the quote that you selected.

   ....
   ....
   ....
   ....

3. How will apply what you learned to your life? Be exact.

   ....
   ....
   ....
   ....

4. Anything else that needs mentioning?

   ....
   ....
   ....
   ....

CHAPTER FIVE
Climbing Down & Moving On

1. What is the most important quote from the chapter? What stands out to you the most?

   ....
   ....
   ....
   ....

2. Explain why you wrote the quote that you selected.

   ....
   ....
   ....
   ....

3. How will apply what you learned to your life? Be exact.

   ....
   ....
   ....
   ....

4. Anything else that needs mentioning?

   ....
   ....
   ....
   ....

CHAPTER SIX
The Bottom of the Mountain

1. What is the most important quote from the chapter? What stands out to you the most?

   ....
   ....
   ....
   ....

2. Explain why you wrote the quote that you selected.

   ....
   ....
   ....
   ....

3. How will apply what you learned to your life? Be exact.

   ....
   ....
   ....
   ....

4. Anything else that needs mentioning?

   ....
   ....
   ....
   ....

CHAPTER SEVEN
Expecting Mountains

1. What is the most important quote from the chapter? What stands out to you the most?

   ....
   ....
   ....
   ....

2. Explain why you wrote the quote that you selected.

   ....
   ....
   ....
   ....

3. How will apply what you learned to your life? Be exact.

   ....
   ....
   ....
   ....

4. Anything else that needs mentioning?

   ....
   ....
   ....
   ....

CHAPTER EIGHT
Another Mountain Awaits

1. What is the most important quote from the chapter? What stands out to you the most?

   ....
   ....
   ....
   ....

2. Explain why you wrote the quote that you selected.

   ....
   ....
   ....
   ....

3. How will apply what you learned to your life? Be exact.

   ....
   ....
   ....
   ....

4. Anything else that needs mentioning?

   ....
   ....
   ....
   ....

CHAPTER NINE
The Next Level: Using your Past Journeys to Become a Greater You

1. What is the most important quote from the chapter? What stands out to you the most?

   ....
   ....
   ....
   ....

2. Explain why you wrote the quote that you selected.

   ....
   ....
   ....
   ....

3. How will apply what you learned to your life? Be exact.

   ....
   ....
   ....
   ....

4. Anything else that needs mentioning?

   ....
   ....
   ....
   ....

CONCLUSION

1. What is the most important quote from the chapter? What stands out to you the most?

   ....
   ....
   ....
   ....

2. Explain why you wrote the quote that you selected.

   ....
   ....
   ....
   ....

3. How will apply what you learned to your life? Be exact.

   ....
   ....
   ....
   ....

4. Anything else that needs mentioning?

   ....
   ....
   ....
   ....

www.ingramcontent.com/pod-product-compliance
Lightning Source LLC
Chambersburg PA
CBHW071347080526
44587CB00017B/2996